The Book of Jude

By Fred DeRuvo

The Book of Jude

Copyright © 2011 by Study-Grow-Know

All rights reserved. Written permission must be secured from the publisher to use or reproduce any part of this book, except brief quotations in critical reviews or articles.

Published in Scotts Valley, California, by Study-Grow-Know
www.studygrowknow.com • www.studygrowknow.tv • www.studygrowknowblog.com

Unless noted, Scripture quotations are from the New American Standard Bible, Copyright ©1960, 1962, 1963, 1968, 1971, 1972, 1973, 1975, 1977, 1995 by The Lockman Foundation.

Cover design by Fred DeRuvo

All images unless otherwise noted were created by Fred DeRuvo

Cover Image by:
Noah's Ark © James Steidl - Fotolia.com

Oneplace.com logo is a registered trademark of Oneplace.com – used with permission.

Edited by: Hannah Richards

Library of Congress Cataloging-in-Publication Data

DeRuvo, Fred, 1957 –

ISBN 0-9837006-9-9
EAN-13 978-0-9837006-9-2

1. Religion – Biblical Commentary – New Testament

The Book of Jude

Contents

Foreword:		5
Chapter 1:	Jude Who?	7
Chapter 2:	Called, Kept, Beloved	13
Chapter 3:	Marked Out	22
Chapter 4:	Unbelievers	38
Chapter 5:	Dreamers & Defilers	48
Chapter 6:	Hidden Reefs	57
Chapter 7:	Enoch's Warning	75
Chapter 8:	Mockers in the Last Day	83
Chapter 9:	Keep Yourselves	94
Chapter 10:	Have Mercy	101
Chapter 11:	Jude's Doxology	106
Chapter 12:	The End	110

The Book of Jude

"To those who are the called, beloved in God the Father, and kept for Jesus Christ: May mercy and peace and love be multiplied to you."

– Jude 1:1-2 (NASB)

Foreword

The book of Jude is only twenty-five verses in length, but it packs a spiritual wallop! Jude, the brother of James (and half-brother of our Lord Jesus), writes a message to believers about the times in which they lived. Those times are not at all that much different from the days in which we now live.

Jude warns against apostasy, licentiousness, and the mockers that are destined to be part of the last days. Even during Jude's day, mocking the Lord's return had already begun. How much worse is it today, roughly 2,000 years later?

In 2011, global society is experiencing many changes and not for the better. All of it points to the fact that this world is moving toward the end of human history. In spite of the obvious signs, people continue to change the gospel, watering it down into a "live as you please" dogma.

People ridicule the Lord and those who follow Him. Laws in society are changing at a very fast pace. It's out with the old and in with the new.

The most tragic part of everything is that within Christendom there are those who mock the Lord's coming, physical return. They say it happened spiritually in A.D. 70. Did it?

What message does Jude have for Christians today? How can we benefit from the wisdom of this man, who wrote hundreds of years ago and could not envision all that we are now experiencing?

In many ways, Jude lays a strong foundation for protecting the gospel, truth that has been entrusted to us by the apostles themselves. Jude also helps us understand that wolves exist among us. They come to us with flattery and false doctrine because they want not only to be accepted by us, but want to gain *from* us.

False teachers and prophets have existed for some time, going back to the days of Moses or earlier. They present a unique problem because of their proclivity to initiate situations that deliberately place them in a positive light.

As our society grows more dangerous because of its denial of God and His truth, we need to be more influenced by Him and His Word. While the enemy of our souls has plans to shipwreck our faith, Jude asserts that by anchoring ourselves to Him and His truth found in His Word, we will be completely prepared for the onslaught of the enemy.

Jude is a book of warning *and* hope. He warns us of the dangers that lie immediately ahead as godlessness continues to increase and urges us onward to the reality of hope we have in Christ Jesus. May the short book of Jude open our eyes to the tremendous truths found within God's Word, truth that makes us free to glorify Him.

Fred DeRuvo, August 2011

Chapter 1

Jude Who?

"Jude, a bond-servant of Jesus Christ, and brother of James" Jude 1:1a

The book of Jude was obviously written by a man named Jude. Who is this Jude? Church tradition attributes this short book or letter to the Jude whose brother was James, who was half-brother to our Lord. This would make Jude Jesus' half-brother as well.

It is likely that Jude chose to identify himself with James, who was understood to be the leader of the church at Jerusalem. This would pave the way for his letter to be accepted more readily than by simply saying that he was the half-brother of our Lord. He didn't want to be seen as capitalizing on the fact that He was half-brother to

Jesus. By doing so, Jude also established the authority for his letter – the reason he wrote it and why it should be heeded.

Please notice that Jude refers to himself as a "bond-servant" of Jesus Christ. At its core, this means that Jude is literally *enslaved* to Jesus. As a slave, Jude willingly does whatever the Master – in this case, Jesus – asks of him.

Because he is a bond-servant, Jude has no mind of his own. He lives to fulfill the will of his Master, Jesus. Someone has wisely stated that the words "no" and "Lord" cannot go together when given an assignment.

We cannot sit back and say, "*No, Lord. I really don't wish to do that. Please don't make me.*" To adopt such a position is to literally *deny* that Jesus is our Lord. In order to truly follow Jesus, we must be willing to go where He would have us go and do what He would have us do.

There is no middle ground here. Jesus Himself states this clearly when He says, *He who is not with me is against me* (cf. Matthew 12:30; Luke 11:23; see also Mark 9:40) and *I wish you were hot or cold, but because you are lukewarm, I spit you out of my mouth* (cf. Revelation 3:16).

The real truth of the matter is that it is incumbent upon each and every authentic Christian to take these words to heart, just as Jude did. Do we consider ourselves to be "*bond-servants*" to Jesus, willing to do whatever it is He commands? Are we completely sold out to Him and His purposes as He was (and remains) completely sold out for our salvation?

While He lived on this earth, Jesus never considered His own needs above the will of God. Daily, moment-by-moment, our Lord offered Himself into the completely capable hands of the Father, depending upon Him to provide what He actually needed, not what He was tempted to *believe* He needed.

Once a person comes to saving knowledge of Jesus, we enter into that life through the narrow gate, from which the narrow road extends. It is called "narrow" for a reason.

First, the narrow gate that leads to a narrow road, which leads to eternal life, is difficult to find. *"For the gate is small and the way is narrow that leads to life, and there are few who find it"* (Matthew 7:14). Why is this gate so hard to find (implied by the fact that "few" find it)? It is because humanity's self-centeredness keeps us from finding it.

Most of us are too selfish to even want to learn about God's things: eternal life, sin, etc. We think we are content to find our own way, but that way only leads to death – eternal punishment (cf. Matthew 7:13).

Finding life eternal is something that requires people to at least be willing to change their opinion about Jesus, something many refuse to do. They believe if they change their minds about Him it will mean that they will have to give up everything they have and become either a monk in some monastery or the Lord will surely send them to the remotest part of Africa as a missionary. It is a lie that the enemy of our souls continues to use because it has worked for so long.

What the Lord wants from us is our life – yes, that is true. However, what we often fail to realize is that He has gifted us with certain talents and gifts that were placed there specifically for Him to use.

For instance, I am a writer. I love to write and I love the study that goes along with that. At the same time, I am creative. I enjoy doing layout and design. When these two gifts are married together, I find that I thoroughly enjoy writing books and creating the covers and interior images that go with them.

I also love to teach and speak before groups of people. These things I believe were given to me by God. They are not things that I gave myself. While I can and have fanned these gifts into a flame by practicing them and doing what I can to make them better, the gifts themselves were given to me.

Maybe you have a gift in the financial area, making you a very good businessperson. Maybe you are gifted musically, playing musical instruments, singing, or both.

Maybe you have the gift of service. You thoroughly enjoy meeting the needs of others, not so that you might get something in return, but so that you will have the satisfaction of seeing someone else's needs met.

These gifts and many others like them are given to us by God. Simply because we become Christians does not mean that all of a sudden the Lord is going to ignore those gifts. He may opt to use them in a way that you do not see coming, but the end result is that you will be far more satisfied when you realize you are using those gifts as God would have you use them, as opposed to simply using them the way you see fit.

Jude considered himself a bond-servant of Jesus. Are you? This is something I must ask myself every day. Am I submitted to His will for my life? Am I asking Him on a daily basis what it is He has for me *now*, *today*?

Jesus constantly stated that He only did what He saw the Father doing – no more, no less (cf. John 5:17-19). What this means is that whatever the Father revealed to Jesus as being His will for Jesus that day is what Jesus did.

This is why there are many times when we wonder just exactly what Jesus was thinking during a particular situation. For instance, when He learned that His friend Lazarus was sick, He did not immediately run to him as we would do. Jesus instinctively knew that there was something special that would result from this situation and if He rushed on over there, the opportunity would be missed.

So by the time Jesus arrived to Lazarus' home, Lazarus had died and been dead and in the grave for four days. This caused Martha to say to Jesus, *"Lord, if You had been here, my brother would not have died. Even now I know that whatever You ask of God, God will give You"* (John 11:21). Through disappointment, Martha reveals her faith in the Lord. She knew that Jesus would hear "yes" to anything He asked the Father if He chose to ask.

The result is that Jesus raised Lazarus from the dead, something no one expected in a million years. This explains why He waited. Had He gone running over, He would have been expected to heal Lazarus prior to his death and the impact and truth of Christ's deity would have been lost on the crowd. It would have simply been another healing.

Arriving four days after He died allowed Jesus to prove His deity to the crowd. Who but God can raise the dead from the grave? No one of whom I'm aware.

Of course, this does *not* mean that if someone in our family is sick, we should waste time getting to them. This was a specific situation in Jesus' life in which He knew the Father was telling Him to wait.

As God the Son, Jesus' thoughts were so in tune with those of the Father (not to mention the fact that they are two Persons of the Godhead) that Jesus could honestly say that He and the Father were one (cf. John 10:30) and before Abraham was, "I am" (cf. John 8.58; see also Exodus 3:14). When Jesus lived His life in the flesh, He became the Father's bond-servant, uniting with Him in purpose and will. This is exactly what we are to do, though we will *never* have the same type of relationship that Jesus has with the Father, simply because we have never been, nor ever will be, God.

Chapter 2
Called, Beloved, Kept

*"To those who are the **called**, **beloved** in God the Father, and **kept** for Jesus Christ: May mercy and peace and love be multiplied to you."* Jude 1:1b-2

The book of Jude opens with a powerful thought. We are *called*. If you are in Christ, which means that you have salvation because you are authentically saved, you have been called.

Too many people argue about whether a person is called or whether a person is meant to never be called. The reality is that everyone who is truly an authentic Christian *is called*. We are called not only to receive salvation but to participate in anything that is connected *to* that salvation. The reality here is that Jude is saying that God has called us.

God is the One who precipitated the call that got our attention, that enabled us to see the truth, and that caused us to embrace that truth. It was because of this that we know we are called.

This calling is something that I'm not sure we focus on all that often. What does it mean to be called?

Think about when you were in grade school or high school. You and your friends stood there while two captains divided up teams by calling on people they wanted on their team. There you stood, hoping that someone would call you before you wound up being the last person. You also wanted to be called by the person you thought was the greater captain.

When you apply for a job that you really want, you often sit by the phone after the interview because you are so anxious to be called. You really want that job and hope it comes quickly.

With God, there is no sense that the last person to come into the fold is any less important than the first one to have received salvation. God calls the entire world to come to Him for salvation. Few will do so, for any number of reasons.

Being called by God is a very personal thing, and we must begin to realize it. We need to dwell on it. It is easy to simply run over these words written by Jude as if they do not hold any real truth or something of great consequence. But consider that God has called us!

So what have we been called *to*? Aside from the aforementioned salvation, we are called to *follow* Jesus. This means many things to many people, but ultimately, the Bible indicates that to faithfully follow Jesus we endeavor to do all that He would have us do in the *way* He would have us do it. Seems reasonable enough.

Let's go back to the example of being a slave. If I am a slave to Jesus, there is no thought of denying His commands. I don't exercise any right I think I might have to disregard Him because something may seem difficult or because it might not capture my interest.

All I have to do is compare His life to mine and note the difference. There was not a time when He did not do what the Father wanted Him to do. Probably one of the most (if not *the* most) difficult times in Jesus' life was the time just prior to His arrest in the Garden of Gethsemane.

It was in that garden as He prayed that He fought hard to ignore the desires of SELF, and He was 100% successful. The tension was great, so much so that He wound up sweating drops of blood. In His humanity, He was tempted to do what most if not all of us would do: reject God's will and shrink from the coming pain and separation from His Father while He hung on the cross for your sins and mine.

Frankly, I cannot imagine the amount of physical pain, fatigue and exhaustion He dealt with, yet He did that so that we might live. I also cannot imagine how it must have felt to be separated spiritually from the Father for even a moment, something He had *never* experienced. As God, He, the Father, and the Holy Spirit were one, yet triune. As Man, Jesus dealt with the same things that you and I deal with, yet He did so without ever sinning. Because of this, His earthly life was one that was in constant, unbroken fellowship and communion with the Father.

Yet on the cross He would experience a time when the Father would have to pour out His wrath on Jesus as well as turn His back on Him. He had to do this because Jesus became sin for us, in spite of the fact that He Himself never knew sin, never experienced sin, and never followed the dictates of sin, though He was tempted just like we are today.

That is love, and it was this love that caused Jesus to volunteer to do what He did. He literally answered the Father's call to live a life of perfection so that the entire law would be fulfilled, and then He offered Himself as an atonement for us. He was called and was chosen. He answered the call because of His love for us.

When we are called, we are not merely called to receive salvation, though that is obviously a large part of it. We are called to take up our cross and follow Him on a daily basis, just as Jesus – daily – followed His Father's will for Him.

The question then becomes, how can we say that He is our Lord if we are not willing to pick up our cross and carry it as He carried His? Why do we believe, as some teach us to believe, that the Christian should expect to live high off the hog down here? Why should we be yearning for the best car, the nicest-looking home, the largest wardrobe, and to have not only our needs but all our wants met as well?

There are many (*too many!*) within Christendom who teach that Jesus is there to make us happy. They teach that, like a genie, He is there to give us what we wish for, if only we will reach out and believe that He can do for us whatever we wish. When we do not receive our wishes, we are told it is because we lack the faith. Yet when we see Jesus' life, we see a man who literally had no place to lay His head. He took each day as it came, and even when He had to pay the Temple tax, He asked Peter to go on a fishing expedition and take the coin out of the first fish he caught. Jesus had nothing, yet He had everything.

The average Christian today seems more concerned with their 401k, their stocks and bonds and their overall livelihood than they are with getting the gospel to the lost people of this world. Jesus has called us to follow Him.

Yes, He grants salvation to whom He will, but He does expect that we will – in exchange for that salvation – turn our lives over to Him so that He might use our life for His glory. Is that asking too much from someone who held back nothing that we might gain eternal life? I don't think so.

We are called to receive salvation. We are called to follow Him. We are called to pick up our cross, and we are called to ignore ourselves in order to fulfill the Great Commission. This is our calling.

*"To those who are the called, **beloved** in God the Father, and kept for Jesus Christ: May mercy and peace and love be multiplied to you."*

We just spoke of what it means to be *called*. Jude wastes no time in telling us that we are called because we are *loved*. It is difficult for human beings to truly appreciate this kind of love. I'm quite certain I have not yet fully understood it and likely will not until I see my Lord in eternity.

We are *beloved*, which means that we are the object of God's love. He created us in His image, and because of that we are exceedingly valuable. Neither the angels nor anything within the animal kingdom was created in His image, but humanity only. This places us at the highest point of all Creation.

Yet evolutionists and others wish to turn that around, making it appear as if humans are destroying God's world and insisting we should spend more time caring about plants and animals than we do. Because of this, the environmental movement has gotten out of control, causing us to lose jobs to foreign nations because they don't want us to cut down timber in parts of the United States that have been known for logging.

They become upset that a particular owl is endangered and petition the government to protect the land the owl lives on. In doing so, the owl takes on greater importance than people do.

I'm not saying that humanity should use up this planet through wanton waste and destruction. I'm saying there should be a balance, and no animal is more important than human beings.

At the time of this writing, nearly 30,000 children under the age of 5 have already died in Somalia due to starvation and disease because of drought and famine. The problem is exacerbated by Muslim forces that keep international aid out and the victims in. They allow no food to enter the country and allow no victims to leave. They are creating a dead zone.

I do not hear our government or any environmental groups decrying the fate of these children and their parents. Human beings are seen as the interlopers on the planet, disturbing the natural order of the species.

Yet, it is clear from the Genesis record (Genesis 1-2) that humanity was created to *use* and *subdue* the earth for our purposes. We were not meant to abdicate our God-given responsibility by treating animals as if they are more intelligent and therefore more valuable than human beings. This is nothing more than a satanic lie – a lie with the intent to overturn God's created order, replacing it with a cheap imitation and making a mockery of God's Creation.

God loves us, and that love is what prompted Him to become a human being – born of a virgin – while retaining His deity, in order to live a life that was infallible. This perfect, sinless life allowed Him to offer Himself as a propitiation for our sin. Because He was perfect in every way, the offer was acceptable.

God the Son – Jesus – died for humanity. He did not die for angels, nor did He die for animals. He died for people created in His image.

Through His death, we have the opportunity to receive eternal life. Beyond this, the curse that now sits on the entire Creation, including the animal kingdom, will one day be lifted.

There are a good many things wrong with this earth physically and those are the result of the fall of humanity. There are too many things to count that are wrong with society, and those too are the result of the fall of humanity.

Because Satan hates, his goal has always been to destroy whatever God has created. Satan's hate is born of jealousy and has limits. God's love is infinite. His perfect love casts out all fear and creates within us the image of His son so that stamped upon each Christian's own personality is the image of Jesus, an image that will grow and eventually supplant everything within us that stands against Him, which is all summed up in SELF.

Imagine someone loving us so much that He was not only willing to die, but *did* die to satisfy the righteous decrees of the Law. More than that, because He died, salvation became available to all who want to receive it. Anyone who wants this free gift can have it, and all they must do is what Paul says in Romans 10:9-10: *"that if you confess with your mouth Jesus as Lord, and believe in your heart that God raised Him from the dead, you will be saved; for with the heart a person believes, resulting in righteousness, and with the mouth he confesses, resulting in salvation."*

The simplicity of that statement by Paul is what throws people off. They become confused, thinking they are missing something, but God's love has deliberately kept salvation simple so that no one can miss it. People still do, unfortunately. It is too difficult for some to believe, so they think it cannot possibly be true.

But that is God's love at work, wanting no one to perish (cf. 2 Peter 3:9). He is patient, and that should be obvious because of the way He has kept His wrath at bay in spite of the way the world sees Him and constantly attacks Him, His Church, and Israel. He is longsuffering (cf. Exodus 34:6; Numbers 14:18; Psalm 86:15, etc.), yet His patience will eventually come to the end.

God's love is there for all who are willing to open their minds to it and embrace the truth of it. God wants no one to perish, and even one person is too many.

It is because of His tremendous love for us that Jesus became human, lived a perfect life, died a criminal's death, and rose again to new life. If this does not say "love" to us, then nothing really will. Either that or we are simply not contemplating the enormity of it.

*"To those who are the called, beloved in God the Father, and **kept** for Jesus Christ: May mercy and peace and love be multiplied to you."*

What a fascinating statement! We are not only called, but we are beloved (which is *why* we are called) and once we respond by embracing His salvation, we are *kept* for one purpose: *Jesus*.

In essence, then, we *become* the property of Jesus, and if you think that this is taxing or difficult on us, then you do not know Him. Could there be a better *master*? Is there anyone better with whom we could be associated?

Jesus took care of His apostles when He walked this earth. He cared for their needs as well as the needs of thousands of other people who lived at that time. Jesus healed the sick, fed thousands, cast out demons, and, most importantly, preached the gospel to them in order that they might receive salvation.

His love for people went deep as He walked this earth. He cried when His good friend Lazarus died (cf. John 11). His heart went out to the crowds that followed Him. They reminded Him of sheep without a shepherd.

The fact that God would stoop to become part of His own Creation as a human being in order to live a life of absolute perfection is amazing. Yet Isaiah tells us that He shared in some of the downsides of being human.

"He was despised and forsaken of men, A man of sorrows and acquainted with grief; And like one from whom men hide their face He was despised, and we did not esteem Him" (Isaiah 53:3)

As people, we know what it is like to be despised or rejected. We know what sorrow feels like. We certainly understand grief and frustration. While the above verse seems to zero in on Jesus' time during His set of illegal trials and eventual crucifixion, it is clear from the gospels that he was despised by the religious leaders. In other parts of the gospels, the average person rejected Him after realizing that He was merely "the son of Joseph, the carpenter" (Matthew 13:55; John 6:42).

Jesus knew what it meant to be fully human, being tempted just as we are tempted (cf. Hebrews 4:15), yet He remained sinless. I cannot imagine taking temptation to the end without sinning. Jesus did, every time.

Just as He was able to keep Himself completely pure, never giving into sin, He is able to keep us in His care. We are kept for Jesus as the Father's gift to His Son. We will one day be perfect, no longer having the sin nature, which prompts us to sin.

Chapter 3

Marked Out

"Beloved, while I was making every effort to write you about our common salvation, I felt the necessity to write to you appealing that you contend earnestly for the faith which was once for all handed down to the saints. For certain persons have crept in unnoticed, those who were long beforehand marked out for this condemnation, ungodly persons who turn the grace of our God into licentiousness and deny our only Master and Lord, Jesus Christ." Jude 1:3-4

In verses three through four, Jude states the reason he was led to write. Originally, he wanted to write about the salvation that he shared with the believers to whom he was writing. However, the Holy Spirit apparently directed his thoughts instead toward those who had wormed their way into the visible Church but were not really of the fold – not authentic believers.

It is interesting how the Lord works. We start to move out in one direction, and the Lord moves us in another. There is nothing wrong with this. Note that Jude did not struggle *against* the new direction the Lord had placed on his heart. When he says, "*while I was making every effort to write...*" he is not necessarily saying that he was determined to write about salvation and nothing else.

It is likely that under the circumstances that existed at the time, with so much upheaval because of growing persecution from Roman authorities and Jews, finding the time to write at all was very difficult. By this time of the church's history, the tide had begun to turn against Christians. First thought by Rome to be little more than a sect within Judaism, they soon realized, because of the negative reaction of Jews toward Christians, that Christianity was *not* something with which orthodox Jewish individuals agreed.

With people like Paul (Saul, prior to his conversion in Acts 9) chasing down Jews who were believed to have converted to Christianity from Judaism, as well as the fact that Jews in general were opposed to Christians, Rome soon realized that persecuting Christians was in their best interest, since it made Jews happy as well. When Jews were happy, there was little danger of Jewish revolt or treasonous uprisings against Rome.

I believe it is for this reason that Jude says what he does about the reason he initially wanted to write. He was likely becoming hemmed in on all sides, and he himself probably had to deal with a number of apostates such as he warns his readers about. When an apostate enters the church, you can bet that little fires will start all over the place, drawing people away if allowed. These little fires, if left unchecked, will grow into full-blown conflagrations. It is the responsibility of the leaders of that particular assembly to take care of the matter by putting that person out of the fold, if necessary, in order to maintain biblical peace, even if that person happens to be a teacher or pastor.

So it was that Jude wrote. The Holy Spirit obviously impressed upon him the realization that apostates were becoming a problem and that people needed to guard their hearts and minds from the error these false teachers espoused. Apostates needed to be *opposed;* it was extremely important to head off problems before they became monumental, and this is what Jude was trying to accomplish. Like the shepherd who carefully watches not only his sheep, but watches for any sign of danger and takes precautions against that danger, Jude, as a shepherd, was dutifully doing what he could to warn his readers that danger may be near. Maybe that danger had not yet approached, but his readers needed to be aware that there was a good likelihood that they would soon be facing the challenges of dealing with an apostate, if they had not done so already.

Jude's letter was also very clearly a form of encouragement. In it, he tried to help them understand what the apostate "looked" like in terms of their *modus operandi* and how they might approach that local congregation. If they could see this in one of these apostates, they would be able to identify him and take action against him.

A car is very difficult to turn when the motor is off and it is in park. Once the car is started and put in drive, as the operator applies pressure to the gas pedal the car begins to move and turning becomes extremely easy. We can see this same scenario in Jude's writing. As he *began* writing regarding a direction he thought was correct, the Holy Spirit simply nudged him to focus on a different area. This is the mark of an authentic Christian who is eagerly looking for the directing of the Holy Spirit. That type of Christian can "go with the flow" and not be encumbered by confusion because he is open to the Holy Spirit's direction in his life.

Once Jude explained what he had originally intended to write, but that he then was moved to deal with another issue, he is off and running, wasting no time in explaining what these apostates do to gain the trust of those within a congregation.

He first warns his readers that above all things, it is important to "contend for the faith." This means a form of apologetics, but Jude is not talking about *debate*. He is taking about presenting the gospel clearly and in no uncertain terms. If someone in the congregation begins using unfamiliar language with reference to the gospel of Jesus, they should be gently questioned in order to determine their real intent.

We know that members of cults work like this, often employing the exact same terms Christians use, yet their meaning is far different from the orthodox meaning. Once we get down to brass tacks and find the meaning that the other individual is applying to his verbiage, the problem can then be tackled with Scripture.

If the person argues against the truth of Scripture, then he needs to be gently warned. If he insists that he is correct, but is not, then he needs to be put out of that congregation. To allow him to remain, he will simply become a poison that will spread through the entire congregation because of his unwillingness to learn and understand the truth of Scripture.

Striving earnestly for the faith means to *defend* it. Do you know *what* you believe and *why* you believe it? If you don't, then you might unknowingly and unwillingly become party to error. As a Christian, it is not good enough to say "I am saved," and that's it. Salvation is the *beginning,* and our growth *starts* at that point. We will spend the remainder of our lives learning more about God, who He is, and what He is accomplishing in and through us.

If you can look back on your life since becoming a Christian and not notice any real difference between the way you are now and the way you were a few years ago, something is wrong. That something has to do with you and your lack of growth. You haven't grown because you have not studied His Word and you have not spent time in prayer, seeking His will for your life. It's that simple, and it is the number one reason that people get sidetracked by others. It is because they do not know His Word, and therefore do not know Him all that well.

The apostate can easily take advantage of a person in such a condition because that apostate may know a few verses here and there and have the ability to skew Scripture so that they sound like what they are preaching or teaching is correct, but is not. People listening to him may easily fall victim to the apostate because they have no ability to defend the faith, since they really don't know what the faith *is*, according to Scripture.

Stealthy
After Jude declares that our Christian faith needs to be defended at all costs, he explains is that these apostates are extremely *stealthy*. He says that they "crept in *unnoticed*." This is important to understand. How could this have happened?

Unfortunately, in many congregations, as the individual congregants come to know one another, they tend to become *relaxed* and even *comfortable* in their relationships because they believe that they truly do *know* the other people. This creates an informal attitude toward others and engenders joy within the fellowship. Outsiders coming in realize that they get along and their resistance to newcomers lessens because of it.

Apostates look for this type of situation in a church. They know that if the congregation gets along and openly accepts newcomers *without* a critical eye, they have an excellent chance of slipping in unnoticed, and after some time will be able to woo many within the congregation over to their way of thinking. It happens all the time in churches today.

I know one man who stated he was a Jewish believer. He did not like to say he was a Jewish *Christian*, or even that he was a *Christian*. He was Jewish and wanted to be known as Jewish. When he went to church, he wore the Jewish prayer shawl and *Yarmulke* (pronounced *ya-ma-ka*). He also stood during prayer with his hands raised to the ceiling. Of course, because of it, this man was noticed, and people began to be attracted to him. He wasted no time in opening the Scriptures to them. He was very soft-spoken and had an air of authority. He also had no difficulty in disagreeing with someone when they said something that he considered to be wrong, and he did so in a way that was not necessarily an affront to others.

As it turned out, this particular individual made it a habit to go around to different Christian churches so that he could *gather* people to himself. He would then form his own Bible study groups and those people would begin to support him through donations (he had formed a non-profit for himself).

As you can imagine, because his actions were done without the knowledge or consent of the leaders of these churches, it became a problem when discovered. This man often taught things that were against the teachings of the particular church from which he gathered people. People were to call him "rabbi" or women were to call him "lord."

One church was forced to call him and explain to him that before he came back (he was a somewhat regular attender), he would have to speak with the Elders to explain his actions. He never went back.

The people that he had gathered from that church were also contacted and told that they had to choose one or the other, to follow that man or continue to associate with the church. It is easy to see why the Elders made this very wise choice. While it sounds like an ultimatum (and it is), the reality is that because that man was teaching things that went against what the church those folks belonged to taught, problems would arise in short order.

Eventually, the man left the state after indicating that he had been called to a Jewish Messianic congregation in the eastern part of the United States. After he left, things went back to a sense of normalcy.

It is very easy to see how this could happen. For one thing, as noted, people today do not read their Bibles, nor do they study it. They depend on the pastor or some other leader or teacher to expound the Scriptures on Sundays and they think that's all they need. Of course that is untrue. We cannot *ever* get enough of God's Word, and needless to say, the more we *know*, the more we *grow*. The more we grow, the less likely we are to fall prey to some apostate wandering through our congregation. This was Jude's main concern, placed on his heart by the Holy Spirit.

Marked Out
Jude also says that these individuals are not only crafty and clever in the way they *infiltrate* a congregation, but they have been marked out long ago for condemnation. In other words, the leaders in the congregation should not hesitate to deal with them firmly if need be, since the apostates are ultimately objects of wrath. It is more important to ensure the safety and solidity of the congregation than to allow someone who lives by *SELF* to thwart God's purposes.

We can see this in action several times throughout the New Testament. Of course, we also note that God dealt with the matter often in the Old with respect to the unbelievers in Israel.

In the book of Acts, chapter five, we learn of a situation in which two people, Ananias and Sapphira, wound up lying to the Holy Spirit. They had sold land and brought the money to the apostles (Peter) so that it could be used to help those in need within the church. Unfortunately for these two, they had gotten together and decided that they would only give *part* of the money they had earned after selling their land to the church, but would still say that they were giving the *whole* amount.

When they gave their money to Peter, the Holy Spirit enlightened Peter so that he knew their plan and was prompted to ask them if the money they were giving was the total they received for the sale of their property. Ananias answered that it was (Sapphira was not with him at that moment). Peter asked Ananias why he thought it was fine to lie to the Holy Spirit. Peter clarified for Ananias that ultimately, he had lied to God, not him (Peter). At that very moment, Ananias fell dead.

Shortly after the men had buried Ananias, Sapphira entered, and Peter asked her the same question. She also answered as her husband had, and also fell dead. The same men who had just finished burying Ananias arrived just in time to remove Sapphira's dead body for burial.

Imagine if these two individuals had been allowed to get away with their lying. It was not important that they gave *everything* to the church. The problem was that they lied about what they *did* give. They could have honestly said to Peter that they sold their property and were giving only *part* of it as a donation to the church. That would have been fine, as they were under no obligation to begin with to give *anything* to the church. They went above and beyond the requirements by deciding to sell the land and offer even part of it to the newly formed and growing Church. It was because they *lied* about the true amount they gave to the Church that God took their lives. This became a warning for all in the Church.

Now, the big difference between Ananias and Sapphira and all the apostates that Jude is referring to is that on one hand, apostates are not truly part of the authentic Church, whereas Ananias and Sapphira *could* have been and likely were part of it. If so, God merely took Ananias and Sapphira home *early*, before they should have died, because of their sin of lying to God – as if He would never know.

Apostates, on the other hand, are not only *not* part of the authentic Church, but really have no *desire* to *be* part of it. Their only desire is for *themselves,* and they will use whatever means necessary to gain what they believe they need and want.

An excellent example of this today can be seen in the lives of many TV and radio preachers. When looking below the surface and past their Christian-sounding verbiage, it becomes clear that money is their god and they do whatever it takes to gain more of it, even using the gospel as their chief means.

I could easily name names, but you may be thinking of the same type of person that I am thinking of here. Look at the TV evangelists who have these large non-profit corporations. They dress in the best suits; they have huge homes on acres of land somewhere, with horses, cattle, and all the rest. How does that work, one might ask?

Many of these individuals teach and preach that they are no different from us, except that they have learned to put their faith to good use. Sure they have, in feeding and catering to themselves. They tell us that we can be just like them if only we will begin to trust God.

The reality is that these people are charlatans and do *not* want us to become just like them because then there will be one less person to support them and their lifestyle. Oh sure, occasionally they will have someone on their show who purportedly has learned to use his or her faith the way they do, but more often than not, these people are plants, designed to encourage the listeners to believe that Joe or Jane Average can exercise faith like the TV evangelist, and look what happens! It's all a terrible sham.

These individuals are apostates because they are using religion to acquire things that they want in life. When you see them in a one-on-one interview, they *appear* humble, they *quote* Scripture, and they *talk* about God as if they truly know Him, but inwardly, they are wolves, merely pretending to be sheep. Over time, they have become masters at deception, and their net worth proves it.

I am *not* saying that God never causes any of His children to become rich. There are many Christians who are wealthy through hard work and God's blessing, and they use their resources wisely for God's Kingdom. There is nothing wrong with that.

I'm referring to people who use *religion* as a means of becoming rich. In God's Name, they *fleece* people, most of them poor already, out of what they have, and they have absolutely no remorse about what they do.

There are many evangelists within the Word of Faith movement, for instance, who do this. They preach a "name-it-claim-it" type of theology in which all we have to do is use our faith to *draw* the things we want/need to us and God will *have* to do it. This is absolute garbage and it is the highest insult to God's sovereignty and holiness, reducing Him to the level of some genie in a bottle.

The reason many succumb to it is because they do not know the Scriptures themselves but simply rely on what these TV evangelists say on the air or write about in their books. The problem, of course, is that for the most part, what these individuals teach is largely taken out of its original context and therefore made to say something else entirely in order to prop up their lifestyle as being the "correct" way to live the Christian life.

I will never forget one time I was watching the Larry King Live show. His guest was Tammy Faye Baker (long before she and Jim had divorced and she had become ill due to cancer). King asked her: if Jesus was alive today, would He be wearing (at the time) $500 suits? Would He live like a millionaire in large homes and have expensive cars? Without hesitation, Baker responded that she believed He would and that He would be a "man of the times."

This is patently ridiculous. He could have easily been a "man of the times" during His own lifetime. The Pharisees and Sadducees were wealthy, most beyond measure. They wore the nicest robes and had the expensive homes and ate the best food. Jesus *could* have done that if He had wanted to compromise, but He didn't want to because it was not the Father's will for His life. Moreover, much of the money that the Pharisees gained was gotten through cheating fellow Jews.

If Jesus were physically alive on this planet today, He would live a life of simplicity, just as He did when He walked this earth over 2,000 years ago. Nothing about Him would be different.

It is tragic that people give so much credence to TV evangelists and others who preach a lifestyle that stands in direct opposition to God's Word. More than anything, God has made authentic Christians *rich* but those riches are in the *spiritual* realm. There is nothing greater than that because all wealth will one day disappear.

Those who live their life piling up riches for themselves will learn that they cannot enter the next life with one penny of it. It doesn't matter to apostates because their ultimate goal is to be surrounded by people who essentially worship *them*, not God, and *give* to them, not God.

Most of these apostates want to become wealthy, but not all. Some are simply content to have many people following their teachings and hanging on their every word. After a time, anything that leader does is fine, even if it means having sexual relations with young girls, or forbidding any of his followers to have sexual relations at all (even if married), or only allowing people to marry the people he approves.

Apostates *need* people to follow them, and it is for this reason alone that they become part of local churches. They are completely aware of the fact that most people who attend churches do not read their Bibles but simply depend upon the teaching of another person to spoon feed them their theology. Apostates know that it is relatively easy to take advantage of members of any flock because of this lack of biblical knowledge.

For the most part, all they have to do is enter into a congregation with a seeming innocence and self-deprecation, yet with an open friendliness that they know will break down barriers. Toss in a couple of memorized Scripture verses and they are in. Once they are accepted by members in that group, they begin to plant seeds, seeds that will take root and eventually cause people to start following the apostate. This occurs over time and is much like the frog that sits in a pot of water that slowly comes to a boil. The frog has no clue that it will eventually boil to death.

If an apostate came into a church congregation and on his very first Sunday ran up to the pulpit and declared himself to be a god, people would escort him out very quickly. Apostates are not stupid. They do not do this, but rather take their time to ensnare certain individuals that have let their guards down, and they build from there.

Turning Grace into Licentiousness
One of the things that these apostates do is start planting the idea that *because* of God's grace, Christians can live any way they want to live. We have been *forgiven*! Because of that forgiveness, all of our sins, past, present, and future, are gone! Since that is the case, then we should enjoy life to its fullest *now*. Come on, join the fun!

Normally, the average church has rules of some sort. Many of these rules are not written down, but the expectation is there and people are aware of those expectations. For instance, we know that the Bible teaches that it is wrong to commit adultery. That's a given, yet people still do it. Aside from the commandments, though, there are rules that churches have that leaders expect parishioners to follow for the good of the entire congregation.

Things like refraining from drinking alcohol or attending movies may not be part of the written dogma of a particular church, but everyone who attends that church knows that it may be frowned upon by the leaders.

Is there anything wrong with actually drinking or going to movies? Some people believe that the Bible teaches that you should never drink. Others don't see it that way. What is the guiding factor? Paul tells us that if what we are doing causes a brother to stumble, we shouldn't do it, and certainly not in front of that brother (cf. Romans 14).

So the guiding parameter here is based on *love* for that other individual. It's part of the Christian's moral code, and Paul details it for us in 1 Corinthians 13.

The apostate teaches people that these things should be enjoyed and *not* prohibited. People tend to like this, and those who are weak in these areas will be drawn to such a person.

I know a number of pastors (and you probably do as well) who have lost their pastorates because they committed adultery with someone in their church, or they were involved in other questionable activities. Either they were counseling the woman and things got way out of hand or they simply found themselves attracted to the church secretary and, over time, went with their desires.

These things happen because people are not close to God. They begin catering to themselves and find ways to keep SELF happy. This is what the apostate does and teaches others to indulge in as well.

The apostate is always happy, always loud (once you get to know them), always has an answer about things biblical, and always encourages people to live life to the fullest. We are *saved;* therefore, since we cannot lose our salvation, go for it! This is a sham.

Yes, I *do* believe a person who authentically receives Jesus as Savior and Lord *cannot* lose that salvation. At the same time, it is important to understand that the Holy Spirit who takes up residence in our life will begin directing our steps and remolding our character in the image of Jesus. If we oppose that, the Lord reserves every right to take us home, just like Ananias and Sapphira.

The people who *say* they are Christians and are really *not* have little to fear in this life. God will likely not "take them home"; that will happen soon enough, when they die and are sent to hell because of their life and actions *now*. The tragedy is what they do to others.

Anyone can *say* they are Christian and many people do. This does not mean that they actually *are* or *were* authentic Christians. It simply means they *said* they were one.

Not long ago, tragically, a madman gunned down nearly 100 people in Norway. He had a page on a social network in which he stated he was a "Christian" and a "right-wing conservative." He also stated that he was part of the Knights Templar.

On the day of his massacre, he was wearing a police uniform so that the young people at the youth camp he was at would not be afraid of him and would even gather round him. It was because of his fake identity as a law enforcement official that he was able to kill as many people as he did that day. He says he's not insane and that what he did he intended to do for the sake of his nation because of his disagreement over Norway's immigration laws and the growth of Islam there.

As you can imagine, the liberal media had a heyday with this news that he was "Christian" and a "right-winger." The actual truth of the situation is that he is *not* a Christian any more than Judas Iscariot was a Christian. That did not interest the liberal media, though. The gunman *claimed* to be a Christian, so we should believe him, right?

According to the liberal media, *yes*. I noticed, though, that this same media did not for a moment believe him to be an actual law enforcement official, even though he attempted to pass himself off as one. Christian? *Yes.* Police officer? *No.* That makes no sense, except for the fact that it merely proves that the average person does not know what constitutes an authentic Christian. Just ask anyone who claims to be an "ex-Christian." They don't know either, but claim that they *were* at one time a true Christian, but now are not.

Apostates are just like this. They *pretend* or *say* they are something when they are not. They have their own agendas and that's all they care about. Pulling the wool over as many eyes as possible is their initial goal so that their ultimate goal can be achieved: serving SELF.

Please notice also that Jude clearly makes the following statement about these apostates: the apostates *"deny our only Master and Lord, Jesus Christ."*

Jude's wording here is important. They not only deny God (Jesus), but notice how Jude refers to Jesus here, as "Master" and "Lord." At the beginning of his letter, Jude called himself a "bondservant," literally, a *slave* to Jesus, and Jude is one *willingly*. He was devoted to Jesus and had *voluntarily* put Jesus in the place of Master and Lord of his (Jude's) life. This is exactly how all of us are to respond to Jesus. We can do it willingly now, in this life, or we will be forced to bend the knee in the next life (cf. Philippians 2:10). Obviously, to do so of our own volition in this life is the hallmark of an authentic Christian. Those who refuse to bend the knee to Jesus *now* will be the ones who are forced to do it *then*.

Apostates like to give the *impression* that Jesus is their Master, while the truth of the matter is that they *deny* Him that place of honor. In effect, the apostate is his own highest authority, bowing to no one else in this life. He believes he answers only to himself and no one else. Again, though, impressions are important. The apostate *wants* above all things to give the impression that he is one of the true flock and other Christians have nothing to worry about, and they can therefore readily receive him with open arms.

Paul also points this out in his second letter to Timothy. He says that individuals like the ones Jude describes are *"lovers of pleasure rather than lovers of God— having a form of godliness but denying its power"* (2 Timothy 3:4-5). Ultimately, these apostates love pleasure, not God, because they love themselves. In order to have a lifestyle which allows them to *indulge* their pleasures, they must have followers who are willing to support their lifestyle. Christians can become easy prey to individuals like this, and it is all because too many do not *study to grow through knowledge of God's Word*.

Chapter 4

Unbelievers

"Now I desire to remind you, though you know all things once for all, that the Lord, after saving a people out of the land of Egypt, subsequently destroyed those who did not believe. And angels who did not keep their own domain, but abandoned their proper abode, He has kept in eternal bonds under darkness for the judgment of the great day, just as Sodom and Gomorrah and the cities around them, since they in the same way as these indulged in gross immorality and went after strange flesh, are exhibited as an example in undergoing the punishment of eternal fire." Jude 1:5-7

Once again, it is amazing to note just how much Jude packs into his short letter. As with any part of Scripture, the more times you read it, the more you gain *from* it. It is a gem because of how much it reveals in such a short amount of space.

After introducing the truth about apostates – men long before marked out for condemnation – Jude refers to several situations from the Old Testament to provide examples for his readers. Jude takes the time to paint pictures so that those in receipt of his letter will more easily see how apostates work.

Out of Egypt
The first such example references God leading the people out of Egypt under the leadership of Moses in order to become His chosen nation of Israel. Though commentators believe somewhere in the neighborhood of 600,000 individuals *left* Egypt with Moses, many were later judged to death by God for their continued unbelief. Though they joined Moses in the journey to the Promised Land, their unbelief kept them from being truly part of that nation.

The idea here is that the people whom God felt it necessary to destroy *never* believed. They were *not* believers one day and unbelievers the next. They *never* believed at all. This is true of many Jews today who live in Israel; they are there for social or political reasons, yet God will ultimately take for Himself a Jewish remnant (Romans 9-11) from that nation and will fully and eventually restore Israel to all of the as yet unfulfilled promises originally given to them.

So if these individuals who came out with Moses never believed, why did they leave with Moses in the first place? It is simply because they were tired of slaving for Pharaoh and living under the extremely difficult conditions Pharaoh created for them. They wanted out of Egypt and so they thought hanging out with Moses was a great idea – until the going got rough. They thought that the Promised Land was right around the corner with easy sailing to get there. Unfortunately, they were wrong, and it was their unbelief that made them wrong.

All of these folks saw the many miracles that God performed through Moses, including the parting of the Red Sea. They saw the cloud by day and the pillar by night, which kept the hot sun off them during the heat of the day, and kept them from freezing at night as they traveled through the desert.

In spite of these and many other miracles that God performed for His nation, many *grumbled*. They wanted a life of ease. They simply wanted God to give them what they wanted and not have to worry about "payback." They didn't want to deal with the sacrificial system. They complained about all the laws. There were not simply ten of them, but 613! While many of these laws were laws that only the Levites (priests) were obligated to follow, there were plenty of laws left over that *all* were required to uphold.

God didn't simply take a people out of Egypt, create a nation from them, and was then going to do *everything* for them like some genie in a bottle. God had a *plan,* and that plan was to create a nation as the foundation of His plan of redemption, through which the coming Messiah would be born into this world. Once born, He would do His job of upholding every aspect of the law, making Him worthy to offer Himself for the sinfulness of humanity after roughly three years of public ministry. I think it is interesting that Jesus was found *worthy*. Revelation 5:6-9 tells us how Jesus, the Lamb, was found to be worthy.

"And I saw between the throne (with the four living creatures) and the elders a Lamb standing, as if slain, having seven horns and seven eyes, which are the seven Spirits of God, sent out into all the earth. And He came and took the book out of the right hand of Him who sat on the throne. When He had taken the book, the four living creatures and the twenty-four elders fell down before the Lamb, each one holding a harp and golden bowls full of incense, which are the prayers of the saints. And they sang a new song, saying,

"Worthy are You to take the book and to break its seals; for You were slain, and purchased for God with Your blood men from every tribe and tongue and people and nation."

In the above section of Scripture, we learn that the Lamb – *Jesus* – was able to take "the book" (the title deed to earth), and please notice that He gave it to the One who sits on the Throne. Notice also the reaction of the four living creatures and the twenty-four elders. They fall down and sing that the Lamb was worthy to take the book and break its seals to open it. Breaking the first seal, by the way, begins the Tribulation period of seven years.

But what is the meaning of the word "worthy"? Jesus was found worthy enough to die for sinful humanity. Who among us would want that job? Yet *"for the joy set before Him endured the cross, despising the shame, and has sat down at the right hand of the throne of God"* (Hebrews 12:2b).

Jesus became worthy because He upheld every aspect of the Law, never deviating from its requirements. In this, He pleased the Father every step of the way.

Moreover, when He came to the time in His life where the cross loomed large before Him, Jesus looked *past* the pain and torture of the cross (both physically *and* spiritually) and saw the joy it would bring to untold millions who would place their faith in Him for salvation. This would then be the catalyst for God to be greatly glorified.

This joy was what prompted Him to do what He did for *us*. This infinite love went on display not only in His life but supremely in His death and the shedding of His blood for all who wish to come to Him in faith and humility. Because of His perfection, death could not hold Him, and He rose, with prisoners in His train (cf. Psalm 68:18).

The people who came out of Egypt and who were ultimately killed by God had not one ounce of faith in them where God was concerned. They were along for the ride because they thought this would be far better than anything they experienced in Egypt. They were wrong, and their constant complaints and even their inordinate desire to go back to Egypt was telling. The journey was not only physically demanding but required strength of faith to rely on God's promises *through* Moses. People who lacked the faith because they were not true believers acted just like apostates do today.

From speaking of those without faith from Egypt, Jude moves on to reference the angels who fell. Of course, there is great disagreement over what these angels *did* which caused them to fall to the extent that God felt it necessary to keep them chained in darkness. This reference does not obviously refer to all fallen angels, and these particular angels are then *not* the demons that roam free now.

Obviously, these angels did something tremendously horrific, something that if left unchecked would have had severe consequences on God's plan of redemption. Some commentators believe that somehow, these angels were able to have sexual relations directly with human women. As a result, the Nephilim were born (cf. Genesis 6). These hybrid creatures were terrifying warriors because of their strength and impossible height.

Others believe that these angels completely possessed human men who then procreated with human women, and that action resulted in the same hybrids we call Nephilim. Whichever the case, the actions of these particular angels were not only unforgiveable in God's eyes but required a sentence so severe that they would not escape and would remain where they were placed until the Day of Judgment.

Some commentators also believe that when Jude speaks of these angels simply abandoning their "proper abode," he is referencing their original state in heaven, before they fell. When they fell by following Lucifer (who became Satan), they abandoned their "proper abode." If that was the case, it would apply to *all* angels who fell. In that event, all angels who fell would have been placed in eternal chains of bondage. The result would be that there would have been no demons during Jesus' day or in ours.

That these angels found some way to co-habit with human women seems to be the likely meaning here. The reason angels would want to do this, of course, would be for the purpose of destroying the pure human DNA that existed when God created Adam. If this DNA could be destroyed, the chance of God becoming man through the human birth process would not occur. However, from the Scriptural record, it is clear that God then kept Noah for Himself and through Noah and his family saved the human race. Noah was the only one considered to be righteous at the time.

By the way, it is interesting to note that Jude is very likely referring here to *The Book of Enoch*, a book that details these particular angels and the story of how they fell. We also read the narrative regarding the Lord's decision to chain and bind them in eternal darkness. It is clear from Peter's second letter that he is also referencing the same situation from *The Book of Enoch* (cf. 2 Peter 2:4-10). Because *The Book of Enoch* existed during the first century, it is also probable that Jesus had access to it and read it.

The point of Jude's comments here is to reference the fact that these angels – though having started out *in* God's presence – came to a point where they chose to no longer *believe* in His authority or His holiness. In effect, they changed their minds about God. That change, due to a lack of belief, caused them to abandon God for Lucifer. In essence, then, they used their free will to call God a liar and rebelled against Him.

Who knows if these angels ever *really* believed wholeheartedly? It would seem that having absolute free will always leads to rejecting God, unless God steps in and allows a person to see the truth. Once seeing the truth, the person can then embrace Jesus and His salvation, much like the thief on the cross did as he hung dying next to the Author of Life (cf. Luke 23).

But we need to differentiate between these specific angels who fell and likely found a way to procreate with human women and the other angels who fell but did *not* participate in that sin. This sin was so abhorrent to God that He locked these particular angels away until they would be judged at the Great White Throne Judgment. The other angels were allowed to continue to roam the earth and the air above the earth as Satan's minions.

From this example, Jude then refers to Sodom and Gomorrah, twin cities on the plain (now believed to be buried under part of the Dead Sea). Homosexuals argue that the sin of the men in Sodom and Gomorrah was *not* being gay and having sex with other men. They believe that it was simply *lusting* after men or women and not treating others with kindness. If that was the case, then God would have destroyed the entire world a long time ago.

Some believe that the men of Sodom and Gomorrah practiced a known custom that, while acceptable in their cities, was not acceptable in other cities. That's bunk. It's a lot of hullabaloo trying to present lies as truth.

It seems clear from various portions of Scripture like Genesis 19:4-5; Leviticus 18:22, 20:13; Romans 1:27; 1 Corinthians 6:9; 1 Titus 1:10 and here in Jude that homosexuality is a perversion of God's intentions for men and women. It is wrong and there is really nothing else to say about it. While gay people disagree – and that's their privilege – the reality is that God's Word seems very clear on the issue.

But here again, Jude is pointing out the problems with individuals like those who lived in Sodom and Gomorrah and who wanted nothing more than to be involved in *constant* homosexual relationships and one-night stands. They lived for it. Today, Gay groups try to tell the world that they are just like heterosexuals and should be allowed to marry. That's all they want to do is to marry, raise a family, and have a loving home, just like heterosexuals get to do. They want their lifestyle to be seen as normal. Unfortunately, for the authentic Christian, that's impossible.

What gays and lesbians perpetrate is a lie, and those who have come out of the homosexual lifestyle can vouch for it. For homosexual men, the main objective is to have homosexual sex as often as possible with as many partners as possible. The fact that the men of Sodom wanted to "know" the angels who had come to whisk Lot and his family away is telling. This "knowing" here is the biblical reference to sexual relations. It is clear that a one-night stand was something the men of the town wanted to indulge in with the angelic visitors.

Anyone who has ever heard of the event called "Up Your Alley" in San Francisco would have to admit that what goes on there – under the guise of being a fundraiser for a good cause – is perversion at its highest level, with various sex acts occurring right in the open! "Up Your Alley" is nothing more than modern-day Sodom and Gomorrah. Because God has not destroyed San Francisco yet does not mitigate the nature of the offense committed by those who live for the homosexual lifestyle without concern.

The argument about being allowed to marry is nothing but a smoke screen. The more states there are that allow that to happen, the more we will then see gays and lesbians wanting something else. It is simply a ploy to see gay and lesbian relationships as normal. Beyond this, we will see a divorce rate take shape in the homosexual community just as we have in the heterosexual community. When that happens, homosexuals will say that they are as imperfect as heterosexuals, so no one should be surprised. The more God gets tossed out of society, the more Satan and his anarchy comes home to roost (cf. Romans 1).

The homosexuals in Sodom and Gomorrah did not believe in God. They wanted nothing to do with Him. Because of this *and* their peculiar sexual proclivities, they treated one another terribly. They were not just having sex with other partners of the same sex (and that by itself is not okay with God), but they were doing far worse, which will not be mentioned or dealt with in this book. Readers are welcome to do their own research.

Since they wanted nothing to do with God, God at first gave them over to themselves and then finally destroyed them. Apparently, there was a great deal of viciousness and cruelty in Sodom and Gomorrah along with the strong sexual appetite that existed. God's purpose in raining down fire and brimstone (rocks with a high content of sulfur that burn easily) was certainly to destroy those individuals, but there was a *greater* purpose as well.

Jude tells us that the destruction of the two cities of Sodom and Gomorrah *"are exhibited as an example in undergoing the punishment of eternal fire"* (Jude 9). In other words, God wanted this destruction of Sodom and Gomorrah to serve as notice to all of what awaited everyone who failed to submit themselves to God and receive His salvation.

I cannot really imagine what this destruction looked like, but I have a book in which we learn of a small, roundish tablet that was found. It has taken years to decode, but apparently, after finally breaking the code, we learn that it is an eyewitness account of the destruction of Sodom and Gomorrah, written down by someone who was miles away at the time of the destruction. The writer describes giant balls of fire coming down from the heavens and the subsequent black clouds of fire and smoke that came from the ground up. I'm sure it was a horrific sight, one that was not soon forgotten by those who witnessed it. They would have known all about Sodom and Gomorrah, and after seeing its destruction, would have understood that something supernatural had occurred because of the lifestyle of those who lived there.

Certainly, those individuals who witnessed such a catastrophic event would know that it was God Himself sending waves of fiery destruction on two towns that were well known, whose reputation had spread across the plains.

In the Olivet Discourse of Matthew 24, Mark 13, and Luke 21, Jesus referred to the days of Noah *and* the days of Lot. In both examples, Jesus pointed out that judgment came upon them quite unexpectedly, and He used these judgments as an example of what it will be like just prior to His return to earth at the end of the age.

Of course, the reason judgment came so unexpectedly is because the people of Noah's day as well as the people of Lot's day had grown so far from God that they likely did not even think of Him anymore. To them, there was nothing wrong with their lifestyle because their conscience had been seared. They were so far from the correct path that they were unable to hear or see any signs that God may have sent them. Then judgment came and they were completely caught off guard.

Instead of discounting the events of the past as if they are simply a bunch of myths tied together in one *larger* tale, we should view them as warnings for us. We should note that these events happened for a reason, and the reason is to warn us. God loves us and wants no one to perish. However, for those who continue in ruinous rebellion due to unbelief (the hallmark of the apostate), He is left with no choice. Destruction is theirs. On which side are you?

Chapter 5

Dreamers & Defilers

"Yet in the same way these men, also by dreaming, defile the flesh, and reject authority, and revile angelic majesties. But Michael the archangel, when he disputed with the devil and argued about the body of Moses, did not dare pronounce against him a railing judgment, but said, "The Lord rebuke you!" But these men revile the things which they do not understand; and the things which they know by instinct, like unreasoning animals, by these things they are destroyed." Jude 1:8-10

In this section of Jude's letter, he details the *character* of apostates, and he has a lot to say. Remember, apostates are essentially *arrogant* and *egotistical*, signs that are eventually seen even if they first appear to come to a congregation meekly and humbly. After a while, their true nature will be revealed because it will come to the fore.

Jude tells us that these men are *dreamers*. They defile the flesh by involving themselves in physical things that they should not do, and they dream about themselves either in inordinately immoral situations or having a great following of people who literally worship them. These things defile their flesh because they become the things they chase after.

That they are defiled doesn't matter to them because it is their goal in life to pursue the things that make them *feel* good. Since they preach that God is love and that all is forgiven, sin does not matter at all and never comes into the picture. It's the antiquated superstitious belief in an angry God that keeps people from really enjoying life, but God has obviously shown how much He loves human beings! Because of that, He wants us to live life as we were originally meant to live it.

What many people do not understand is that when we become authentic Christians (cf. John 3), we continue to exist with the sin nature within us. We are *not* like our first parents, Adam and Eve, who knew what life was like *before* they chose to disbelieve God.

On our best day, we will not be able to experience that type of life *until* our sin nature is completely removed from our being. Then, and only then, will we experience life as it was truly meant to be lived. We cannot do that now.

This is the lie the apostates preach, and they indulge in their own personal proclivities that they enjoy, encouraging others to do the same thing. Let it all hang out. Go for the gusto! In this way, they are dreamers, trying to create what they *imagine*. Dreams are not real. They are something that our brains conjure up for us when we sleep. When we wake up, we realize instantly that whatever we dreamed while we were asleep was just that, something we dreamed while we slept.

Jude is referring to dreams in another way, though. We all look down the road of our lives and see ourselves in various situations. People have *dreams* for themselves. Some dream that one day, they will be a pro basketball or baseball player. Others dream about having a career in music or acting. Still others dream about owning their own law firm one day. There are many good dreams and many of them are goals to shoot for; however, as Christians we always need to be prepared to recognize that our dreams might not be God's dreams for us.

The apostates – these "dreamers" – dream of ruling over people, having their own needs met, and gaining riches from gullible people who long ago stopped thinking for themselves. They believe that getting there is the key, and it does not matter *how* they get there or who they use.

Not long ago, the leader of a polygamous sect of Mormonism was given a life sentence for having sexual relations with young girls. The sect is known as the *Fundamentalist Church of Jesus Christ of Latter Day Saints,* and Warren Jeffs was/is the only and ultimate leader.

It should be of interest to note that in nearly all examples of various cults and sects, these freakish groups wind up with one person – usually male – who ends up having sex with as many young children as possible.

Jeffs maintains that these were his brides and that they had to have sex with him as part of their "worship." In truth, individuals like Jeffs are child abusers and molesters using religion as a cloak for their illegal and highly immoral activities. This is what false teachers and apostates do, and they succeed because of the gullibility of the people with whom they interact.

Apparently, Jeffs is still in control of his group even though he is headed to prison for 119 years. How he will control the group is not known, but just like criminal gang bosses can and do control their gangs from behind prison walls, it should not be that difficult. I'm sure the FBI and other law enforcement groups will keep their eye on this sect. With Jeffs behind bars, someone else will have to at least step up to lead by proxy. Things may go on essentially as they have been even though Jeffs will not physically be there to lead the group.

Apostates, once again, are concerned *only for themselves*. The people they gather are gathered to fill the needs of the apostate. They cannot have the life they want without people who can do the footwork and donate money. They are smooth operators when it comes to gaining a following.

Consider the adults who willingly allowed Jeffs to have sex with their young girls. What normal parent does this?

It is because of this danger that leaders within every authentic Christian congregation need to be constantly alert. They are charged with protecting the flock and they need to take that job seriously.

Everyone in the local congregation should be on the lookout for these wolves dressed like sheep, but the leaders have the larger responsibility. If they close their eyes or fall asleep on duty, terrible things could happen.

It is interesting that from here, Jude refers to Michael the Archangel and his interaction with the devil over the issue of Moses' body. This incident does not appear in any other place in Scripture; Jude is referring to the account that appears in the *Assumption of Moses*.

Here we learn that after Moses died, prohibited by God from entering the Promised Land (cf. Deuteronomy 34), Satan apparently tried to steal his newly deceased body. Michael the Archangel was sent to respond. God wanted Moses' body buried and Michael carried that mission out. To this day, no one knows where Moses' body is buried, and it doesn't matter either.

The point of Jude's comments here is that even though Michael the Archangel *could* have taken Satan on directly, he instead chose to defer to the Lord and *His* authority. When Satan tried to grab Moses' body and started arguing with Michael about it, Michael simply said, *"The Lord rebuke you!"* and based on our Lord's authority, Satan was rebuked and likely left without saying another word.

Too many times, Christians today believe they are involved in some type of "deliverance ministry" in which they need to come directly against the powers of darkness. I am *not* saying that God does not use Christians to free people from the powers of darkness. I'm not saying that at all.

However, I *am* saying that when we come up against Satan or one of his minions, it is best to rebuke them in the Lord's authority, just as Michael did here in Jude's account. In Luke 10, we read of the 70 disciples whom the Lord had sent out in the authority of His Name to spread the gospel. They came back marveling that even the demons listened to them and had to obey.

These demons obeyed because of the *Lord's* authority, not the individual Christian's authority. Our authority rests only in Jesus. We have no authority apart from Him. It is better for us to realize that as Christians, we have no authority of our own. We operate under the authority of Jesus and it is upon *that* authority that demons tremble and flee, not because of any authority we may think we have in and of ourselves.

The people who actually go *looking* for Satan and his hordes of demons are on the wrong track, in my opinion. Of course, they would disagree with me, but the truth of the matter is that it seems to be little more than some sideshow type of endeavor.

People in general are curious about evil, with demonic possession, with horror of all sorts and can even become enamored with it, kind of like seeing a terrible car wreck and not being able to turn away. Horror movies have always been a big draw for the multitudes. Why should Christians be any different? Many Christians are infatuated with the evident power of the enemy and want to see it in action. I think that's a mistake. For one thing, it is dangerous if the Christian is not a strong believer. For another, the focus is wrong.

Our focus should be on spreading the gospel. In the course of doing *that*, we will likely meet the challenge of dark forces from time to time. It will be enough to rebuke them at that point when it crops up, rather than go on a search looking for demons under every rock and behind every door.

Nonetheless, Jude is noting that the apostates he has been talking about seem to think they have the power to take on the enemy in their own strength. Oh, they won't say it that way. They'll be sure to throw in Jesus' Name from time to time as they weave their web of lies, but they always wind up puffing themselves up.

They are the ones who went against the demon or Satan (in Jesus' Name). *They* are the ones who went head to head with Satan, undeterred and unwilling to back down (in Jesus' Name). It is the apostate who bravely faced the powers of darkness at great risk to himself in order to set some poor soul free.

Some apostates will even turn it into a funny anecdote. *"Oh, I'll tell ya what, people! (CROWD: WHAT?!) I'm glad you asked! (CROWD: laughter). I'll tell you when I started toward that man filled with the power of demons, he began to cower right in front of me! (CROWD: applause).*

"Yessir, this ol' demon, he knew he was no match for me. Why is that? (CROWD: Jesus!) That's right. I'VE got the power of Jesus in ME and there's no demon in the universe that can stand against that!"

At this point, the TV evangelist begins a little "happy dance" on stage, and row by row, people in the audience start clapping their hands and standing. Everyone is just so joyful!

Now wait a minute here. For *whom* are these people clapping, the evangelist or Jesus? I haven't heard the evangelist say anything about this poor soul who was possessed but now *belongs* to Jesus. Did the person become a Christian? I have no idea.

In fact, all I heard was how brave and courageous this evangelist was, and implicit in his discourse is that fact that he is obviously extremely strong in the Lord to be able to withstand the onslaught of the enemy. You definitely want to hang out with him!

In short, it's all about the evangelist, but it *sounds* like it's all about Jesus. Nope, all eyes on the evangelist. Don't you wish you were like *him*? Don't you wish you had God's power coursing through your veins like *he does*? Don't you wish you were as close to God as *he* obviously is to Him? Even devils shudder because of him.

Folks, we don't even know if the story the evangelist just told us actually *happened*! He's a dreamer, a defiler. He goes where Michael the Archangel did not go, and Michael's power is far superior to that TV evangelist's, whose real power is in his ability to brag and lie.

It is because of this –these apostates take the powers of darkness so lightly – that they will eventually be destroyed by these very things, because the web that Satan weaves is extremely *intricate*. He'll let these apostates think they have power over him; all the while he is doing just exactly what they are doing, but to the evangelist.

While that evangelist is reeling people in, Satan is reeling the evangelist in, and the evangelist is not even aware of it any more than the people are aware of what's happening to them. Instinctively, the evangelist should know better, but he ignores that instinct.

I've always grown up around animals and maybe you have too. I love dogs, but ever since marrying my wife, I've grown to love cats, and I never thought that was possible because I have never seen cats as pets. I saw them as animals that just walk around your house without much love and affection.

What is interesting is that I have yet to see a cat with a similar personality to another cat, yet with dogs, they all seem to have basic similarities. Unlike dogs, cats need to adopt *you*. They need to learn to love and trust you before they will accept you into their circle.

We have six cats. Yep, six. A number of them were rescue cats and would have likely died without us or someone nursing them to health. Each cat has his or her own personality, and it can be hilarious at times, or at least intriguing.

We have one cat that my wife wanted for herself, but that cat – Chloe – has adopted *me*. She likes my wife, but she *loves* me. Other cats in our household have adopted my wife.

One cat loves food, and anytime she is stressed, she has to go to her food bowl. Even if she doesn't eat, it gives her a sense of security to know that food is in her bowl. She also has to have her food in one specific place. She can't eat from any other food bowl.

One of our cats likes to play by spinning in circles in the hallway. She does this so that you will notice her, but you're not allowed to *join* her. You can simply watch.

Another cat we have does a head-butting thing, mainly with me. No other cat we have does this and it is the way he shows you he loves you.

Each of our cats have different personalities, yet they all share similar *instincts,* and these are the instincts God gave them. Those instincts keep them alive, or are supposed to do so.

If they are out front and a car or truck comes up the street, they head for the cat door and into the house. One of them – since he was nearly run over by a car when he was younger – heads for space under the nearest bed until the "danger" has passed.

Every animal lives by instinct, and when they follow the dictates of their instinct, it can keep them alive. That's why God gave them instinct: as a means of *survival*. Animals do not make logical decisions, although when they live by instinct, they wind up *being* logical.

However, these apostates *ignore* instinct. They instinctively know that they should not be doing certain things because their conscience points that out. Oh well, they ignore it, no worries. These things will destroy them.

Most know that Rock Hudson was gay, but for years, Hollywood kept that secret well hidden from the public. This is what Hollywood did in the days of the studio system, only allowing the public to see the best side of their contracted stars. Hudson contracted AIDS because he had unprotected sex with someone that he did not know and others had warned him about. They told him to avoid this one man. Hudson did not listen and contracted AIDS, from which he died later.

Those people that were warning Hudson were acting as his conscience. They obviously knew that the risk was great and that he should avoid that particular person. He refused to listen to their sage advice and died because of it. He ignored the dangers, and the very thing he participated in that he seemed to live for killed him in the end.

People who do this wind up acting like unreasoning animals. Animals live by instinct. An animal that pays no attention to instinct will soon come to an untimely death. If human beings do the same thing, why should they be exempt?

Chapter 6

Hidden Reefs

"Woe to them! For they have gone the way of Cain, and for pay they have rushed headlong into the error of Balaam, and perished in the rebellion of Korah. These are the men who are hidden reefs in your love feasts when they feast with you without fear, caring for themselves; clouds without water, carried along by winds; autumn trees without fruit, doubly dead, uprooted; wild waves of the sea, casting up their own shame like foam; wandering stars, for whom the black darkness has been reserved forever." Jude 1:11-13

I love the imagery Jude conjures up here in this section of his letter. He refers to apostates as "hidden reefs" and "clouds without water." These pictures are striking.

Jude begins by issuing a declarative *"Woe to them!"* This is obviously *not* a good thing even if you do not know what a "woe" is all about.

A "woe" is something that is absolutely terrible, and before Jude happened on the scene, the prophets of old used this phrase to warn the people to whom they prophesied what was ahead if they continued in the path they were moving on, *spiritually* speaking.

Cain
Jude is saying that the deepest misery awaits them because they are doing the same thing that Cain did when he killed his brother, Abel. He compares them to Balaam also, who tried on several occasions to curse Israel but was unable to do so because he was stopped by the Lord.

Men like Cain and Balaam do what they want to do for their own personal gain. In Cain's case (cf. Genesis 4:1-15), he killed his brother Abel because he was jealous of the fact that Abel had brought before the Lord the *correct* offering.

Obviously, both men had been taught about sacrificing to God, something that both Adam and Eve had learned directly in the Garden of Eden after they fell when they saw God kill several animals in order to make proper clothing for the two (cf. Genesis 3). There were probably a number of things that God explained to them that day about the sacrificial process, which, of course, was not thoroughly outlined until much later, through Moses.

Adam and Eve passed on this knowledge of the sacrificial offering to their children, and it is clear that Cain – though he brought the wrong sacrifice *deliberately* – knew of it, as did Abel. Cain could have gone to his brother and bartered with him, fruit and vegetables (Cain farmed) for a proper animal for sacrifice (Abel tended flocks). Cain chose not to do this in spite of the fact that he knew he was bringing the wrong sacrifice.

Someone may argue, "*Well, gee, at least Cain brought <u>something</u> to sacrifice.*" That's true, but that is not the point. The fact that Cain brought the *wrong* sacrifice speaks of his own carelessness with respect to any relationship he may have thought he had with God. In fact, what he did, he did simply out of *duty* and *compulsion*, not because he truly wanted to do the right thing in God's eyes. In other words, Cain's heart was far from God. His heart wasn't in it.

The sacrificial system that God first introduced to Adam and Eve was always designed to point ahead to the time of Jesus and His ultimate sacrifice on the cross. He died a terribly painful death, shedding His blood for humanity. While vegetables and fruits are certainly living things, they are no replacement for an animal that bleeds, feels pain, and sheds its blood onto the ground. This type of death pointed ahead to the Passover death of Jesus on behalf of the world.

Cain consciously chose to ignore the ramifications of the sacrificial system and brought vegetables instead of a live animal. Even though Satan was very unlikely to see what the sacrificial system ultimately meant, this was undoubtedly Satan's attempt to downplay the importance of the cross of Jesus.

At this point in time, Satan would not have been able to see ahead into the future to a time when God would become human, live a sinless life and then die for humanity. At this point with Cain, Satan was likely simply tempting Cain to become disobedient and do things his way instead of God's way. That's always the way it is with Satan.

This is the basic attitude in the person who is an apostate. They will deny this to the hilt, and in some cases they are simply unable to see it, but they are completely self-centered, caring only for themselves. The easy way is the *better* way for them. Such was Cain's attitude.

Balaam

Balaam was the same. He tried to tempt Israel into compromising their faith in God by worshipping idols. He did this because he was offered a large sum of money. He wanted the money, of course, but why was he offered the money in the first place?

Numbers 22 tells us that Balak, King of Moab, had seen how the Israelites had dealt with the Amorites. He was naturally afraid because the number of Israelites was so great. He envisioned them one day doing to him and his kingdom what they had done to the Amorites.

So Balak crafts a plan, a plan he hopes will bring the Israelites to the point of judgment by their God. If he (Balak) can somehow convince the Israelites to sin by worshiping idols, then maybe God would judge them, and he and his kingdom would be safe.

So he offers Balaam a hefty ransom to curse the Israelites so that they would compromise and worship idols. Balaam is nearly completely overcome by his greed, and each time he tries to curse Israel, he winds up not being able to do so, blocked in his attempts by God.

All are likely familiar with Balaam and his donkey, because at one point, while riding his donkey to go see Balak in order to curse the Israelites, the donkey stops because an angel blocks her path. At first Balaam is unable to see the angel and starts whipping the donkey to get her moving.

The Angel of the Lord that blocked the donkey's path is given the ability to speak, and then Balaam's eyes are unveiled enough to also see the angel. He realizes the stupidity of his ways and immediately repents.

Ultimately, Balaam is guided by his own greed, which nearly does him in. This is the way of the apostate, who, as has been pointed out, lives his life to please himself and surrounds himself with people who can make his dreams become reality.

Korah
The "rebellion of Korah" refers to Korah the Levite, who led a mutiny against Moses. We read the sad tale in Numbers 16.

"Now Korah the son of Izhar, the son of Kohath, the son of Levi, with Dathan and Abiram, the sons of Eliab, and On the son of Peleth, sons of Reuben, took action, and they rose up before Moses, together with some of the sons of Israel, two hundred and fifty leaders of the congregation, chosen in the assembly, men of renown. They assembled together against Moses and Aaron, and said to them, "You have gone far enough, for all the congregation are holy, every one of them, and the LORD is in their midst; so why do you exalt yourselves above the assembly of the LORD?" (Numbers 16:1-3)

Wow, talk about *arrogance*! Look at the last sentence in the above text. There, Korah – *on his own* – has decided that every person in the camp is *holy*, and from his standpoint, the Lord is with them. He then pointedly asks Moses why he thinks he has the right to "exalt" himself above everyone else.

Well, if I remember correctly, way back at the burning bush (cf. Exodus 3), Moses did *not* want the job that God offered. Moses tried numerous times to refuse it, making a number of excuses to the Lord, and finally telling Him that he stuttered and so wasn't able to be any type of real spokesman for the Lord.

The Lord finally had enough and said that He would give Aaron to Moses to do the speaking for him (Moses) if need be, but Moses was the chosen man whether he liked it or not. During this time in Egypt and after leaving, Moses had put up with quite a lot from those who would become Israelites.

Moses' reaction here speaks to his humility. *"When Moses heard this, he fell on his face; and he spoke to Korah and all his company, saying, 'Tomorrow morning the LORD will show who is His, and who is holy, and will bring him near to Himself; even the one whom He will choose, He will bring near to Himself. Do this: take censers for yourselves, Korah and all your company, and put fire in them, and lay incense upon them in the presence of the LORD tomorrow; and the man whom the*

LORD chooses shall be the one who is holy. You have gone far enough, you sons of Levi!'" (Numbers 16:4-7)

Moses was a humble man, and he knew that what he was doing he did because of the Lord. He was also not above becoming righteously angry as well when the situation warranted it. This situation is reminiscent of the many times that the religious leaders of Jesus' day came to Jesus demanding to see His "credentials."

Moses was under God's direction, and though many within the camp of Israel could not or would not understand God's leadership in and through Moses, the truth is that God was in charge and Moses was simply His servant, carrying out the Lord's wishes. Moses could have asked God to strike these infidels dead, but he chose not to do so. In fact, by the time we get to verse 15, we see that Moses does become fairly angry, but it is a righteous anger because he knows that he has not wronged anyone and he ultimately leaves it in the Lord's hands to decide the outcome. The Lord would decide, and this is exactly what transpired.

Verses 20 through 22 tell us God's response. *"Then the LORD spoke to Moses and Aaron, saying, 'Separate yourselves from among this congregation, that I may consume them instantly.' But they fell on their faces and said, 'O God, God of the spirits of all flesh, when one man sins, will You be angry with the entire congregation?'"*

God was going to hold the *entire* congregation of Israel responsible for Korah's rebellion. Immediately, Moses and Aaron interceded for the congregation. Once again, Moses acts as a type of High Priest, interceding on behalf of the people. Since all the people in the congregation were sinners – even though they had not specifically involved themselves in this particular sin led by Korah – they were guilty nonetheless. God in His holiness could have justifiably destroyed them all and started over with Moses.

Ultimately, God chose to destroy Korah and those who stood with him. There should be no doubt that God had chosen Moses and Aaron, and He would prove it to the Israelites once again.

When Moses finished speaking with God, he spoke to the Israelites. *"Then Moses arose and went to Dathan and Abiram, with the elders of Israel following him, and he spoke to the congregation, saying, 'Depart now from the tents of these wicked men, and touch nothing that belongs to them, or you will be swept away in all their sin.' So they got back from around the dwellings of Korah, Dathan and Abiram; and Dathan and Abiram came out and stood at the doorway of their tents, along with their wives and their sons and their little ones. Moses said, 'By this you shall know that the LORD has sent me to do all these deeds; for this is not my doing. If these men die the death of all men or if they suffer the fate of all men, then the LORD has not sent me. But if the LORD brings about an entirely new thing and the ground opens its mouth and swallows them up with all that is theirs, and they descend alive into Sheol, then you will understand that these men have spurned the LORD.'"* (Numbers 16:25-30)

God had told Moses to tell the people to move away from Korah, Dathan, and Abiram and their dwellings (cf. Numbers 16:24). Moses did this, but also note that Moses goes onto say something very interesting about how Korah, Dathan, and Abiram will die. Obviously, the Lord placed this on Moses' heart when he said that the ground would open up and they would fall in Sheol alive. Let's see what happens.

"As he finished speaking all these words, the ground that was under them split open; and the earth opened its mouth and swallowed them up, and their households, and all the men who belonged to Korah with their possessions. So they and all that belonged to them went down alive to Sheol; and the earth closed over them, and they perished from the midst of the assembly. All Israel who were around them fled at their outcry, for they said, 'The earth may swallow us up!' Fire also came

forth from the LORD and consumed the two hundred and fifty men who were offering the incense." (Numbers 16:31-35)

That is scary! So scary that the people who were *not* part of Korah's rebellion moved even further away from him and his household for fear that they would be affected as well. As soon as the people had separated from Korah, the ground opened up and the text tells us that the earth swallowed Korah, his family, and his group alive and they went directly to Sheol.

As if that was not enough, God sent fire from heaven to destroy the 250 who rose up *with* Korah. They had offered incense (presumably to an idol), and that, along with their rebellion against Moses (and ultimately against God), was enough reason for God to take their lives.

God was building His nation, and He would not stand for rebellion against the man He had personally hand-picked to lead that ragtag, motley group from Egypt to the Promised Land, turning them from that motley crew into a nation that would give birth to the Messiah (cf. Revelation 12). They were to do it God's way, or not at all.

Esau
Again, this is the way of the apostate, the false teacher, who has only his own interests at heart. His pride keeps him from caring about anyone else, and he thinks he is unquestionably correct. He sees no need to be under anyone else's authority and leadership because he himself is a leader. Since the apostate fancies himself a leader, why does he really need anyone else?

This is why Esau became hated by God (cf. Malachi 1:3; Romans 9:13). Esau sold his birthright for a bowl of soup (cf. Genesis 25). He did so because it was more important for him to feed his flesh than understand the importance of his birthright. The oldest son had the birthright, and it was this son that had the relationship with God on behalf of his family. Esau essentially said that a bowl of soup was worth far more than any birthright he may have inherited by being born first. He was really talking about a relationship with God. Pride caused Esau to look at the situation like this, and it was pride that eventually brought the nation Esau founded (Edom) down to nothing shortly after the destruction of Jerusalem and the Temple by the Romans under Titus in A.D. 70. It is interesting to note that according to Psalm 83, we may once again see the rise of the nation of Edom for God's End Time plan, but that's another story.

By the way, as an aside here, it is interesting to note that Esau married one of Ishmael's daughters. Ishmael is the father of the Arab nation, through which Islam came into being.

We read that the woman Esau married was named Mahalath (cf. Genesis 28:9), which also means that even though Edom is gone, modern-day Arabs can trace their roots back to Ishmael through Esau. In marrying into Ishmael's family, Esau cemented his place in history as siding *against* Jacob, his brother, which eventually became the nation of Israel.

Back to Korah
Korah thought that his coup against Moses and Aaron would impress the people, and I'm sure he thought that *he* would become their new leader or that he would be successful in knocking Moses off his pedestal so that the Israelites would be able to live the way they wanted to live. I'd be willing to bet these "men of renown" were ready to take Moses' place in an instant.

Korah did not want Moses to be in authority any longer, and obviously, at least 250 others agreed. In the end, they all died because they were opposed to God, not simply Moses. This is the problem with pride. It may *appear* to be intelligent and meaningful at first, but when it is unmasked and shown for what it is, it is clearly seen that pride attacks God at every turn. It is the *worst* of sins because it is the *root* of most of them.

Those who are filled with pride will do whatever it takes to puff themselves up further in their attempts to reduce God to nothing. Satan was the first to try this and he fell as a result. Adam and Eve were convinced by Satan that they could get out from under God's rule by eating of the forbidden fruit, which would open their eyes, allowing them to see their own inner deity. They obeyed Satan and fell just as He had done. It is for this reason the Scriptures say, "*Pride goes before destruction, And a haughty spirit before stumbling*" (cf. Proverbs 16:18). From pride, nothing good springs forth. It always destroys, and this is reason enough why God hates it.

The apostate often truly believes that his actions, teaching, and demeanor are in line with what God wants, but rarely, if ever, is this the case, and of course his view of God is certainly skewed. Normally, the apostate stands opposed to God, and while some may not realize it, too many apostates know exactly what they are doing.

Hidden Reefs
After providing these three examples of what apostates are like, Jude likens them to "hidden reefs." How apropos is that? Anyone who has a boat or who has gone swimming in the ocean near coral reefs knows how much damage these reefs can cause.

Reefs are beautiful to look at. They are covered with coral of all sorts of colors, and the way they reflect the light is fascinating. The design of a coral reef is also very intriguing, almost beguiling. Because of this, their inherent danger is often hidden. The cut sustained from a piece of coral is akin to being cut with glass. It is not uncommon for a reef to gouge or rip open the hull of a small boat or severely cut a swimmer who is unaware of the reef's presence and accidentally dives onto it.

That's the interesting thing about coral. It *looks* beautiful on the outside and therefore is often attractive to us, but it is *dangerous*. Apostates are often charming people who have an air of intelligence, depth, and *seem* to be genuinely interested in people. All too often, though, people are completely unaware of the danger until they get totally sucked in and wind up under the apostate's control.

Think of Jim Jones, Father Divine, David Koresh, and any other individual like them that comes to mind. Initially, these people were charismatic, acting like magnets to other people. You wanted to be around them because they were fun, exciting, inviting or embracing.

You felt loved. You felt as if the person was supremely interested in you and you alone. That's how people get sucked in: because of the sense of excitement and belonging. It didn't matter that some of what was heard when they preached was not quite right and red flags went off. What mattered is *how you felt*.

Apostates capitalize on this feeling that people have about themselves. They know that most people are insecure to some extent, so if they can find their insecurity then use it to draw that person close to them, the apostate knows that he will be able to pull them in and they will be theirs.

It's no wonder that Jude – though he initially felt compelled to write about salvation – felt it even more important to stress the character of the apostate and the way the apostate worms his way into the congregation *first*, and then into the hearts of the people *next*.

As attractive and inviting as that apostate may be on the outside, he is like a hidden reef, with nothing but danger and disaster waiting for those who bring their boats too close. Once they get to that point, though, it is often too late in most cases, and history has given us that lesson repeatedly.

Love Feasts
The apostate fits right in with the local congregation to such an extent that they sidle up to folks during their love feasts (dinners usually served prior to the Lord's Supper). They blend in easily, and most are not aware that they are there with ulterior motives and are partaking of not only the love feast, but also of the Lord's Supper.

The apostate doesn't care that he is partaking in judgment because his heart is not in the right place when he bows his head in remembering the painful death of our Lord and Savior. This doesn't matter, because like the priests in Ezekiel who worshiped idols in secret so that the Israelites were not aware of it (but God was), the apostate keeps up the façade of being a true servant of God, all the while serving only himself. People like this tend to believe that their secret agenda is safe from all eyes, including God's eyes.

Jude's Description
Jude carries his description of apostates onward, wanting to ensure that his readers get the point. He wants them to know in no uncertain terms how despicable the apostate's actions are as they mingle with the congregation. Jude calls them clouds without water, carried along by winds.

I used to live in upstate New York. It's normally green throughout the year, except, of course, in winter because of the humidity and rainfall. Without the rain, things would look brown, like they do in California during the summer.

Apostates are not like clouds that bring refreshing, life-giving water. They may look like clouds, but they have nothing within them that benefits anyone else.

It is of course even worse when these apostates become leaders in a local church. They often gain these positions because of their charm, their good-natured personality, or their overall charisma and self-assurance.

Once they begin teaching, though their overall appearance and demeanor may *promise* "rain" (spirituality), they often bring nothing. I can think of a number of people who have done great harm in the Name of Jesus because of what they preach. Yet these individuals have a very large following because of their charisma and charm. They normally have large personalities, making it difficult for the average person to disagree with them.

On days when the humidity was high in New York, you always looked for a coming storm, because you knew that the rain would reduce the humidity. It was like letting the air out of a balloon. It normally always felt good.

The clouds that passed overhead and released no water did nothing to relieve the humidity, and in fact, sometimes the humidity seemed to *increase* because of the additional pressure system that clouds can help create. Rain was needed, and clouds that passed overhead and did not have water to release were simply pretty to look at, and that was all.

Jude's next bit of imagery has to do with trees. He describes apostates as *"autumn trees without fruit, doubly dead, uprooted."* Yesterday, my wife brought home fruit from a Farmer's Market near her work. One of my favorite fruits is the peach. My wife likes them crunchy, but I like them ripe and soft. To me, they are far tastier when they are just overly ripe. They also smell wonderful. I love good fruit, whether it's a peach or an orange. If it's good and ripe, then I know I'll enjoy it.

We have an orange tree in our backyard that has been there since we planted it shortly after we moved in twelve years ago. Even though the tree *looks* healthy with nice green leaves and new growth every year, it has not produced a single orange in all that time. It only looks good, but produces nothing edible. It even tried this year, starting to produce an orange that got to the size of a marble, and then it was gone. We've thought many times about uprooting it and getting rid of it since as a fruit tree, it's not doing its intended job.

This is the apostate. While he may appear to be something of quality on the outside, the fact that he produces no real fruit is the key indicator that something is terribly wrong.

We could probably look at just about any church in America and find people who do not produce any fruit. Some of these people are clearly very needy and it is obvious they attend church to have their own needs met and are not at all interested in giving back by using the gifts God gave them to help edify the congregation (if they are authentic Christians).

It may also be that at least some of these people are *not* authentic Christians and are simply there for their own reasons. They may either believe that they are indeed true believers, or they *know* they're not. In the case of the latter, they are likely there for no good reason.

Jude knows how difficult it is sometimes to identify the type of person he is referring to, so he provides many examples and pictures to help leaders narrow down that process. Clouds without rain and trees without fruit are two ways that he endeavors to help people learn to judge the difference so that these apostates become more *noticeable*.

Jude is not done yet. He further defines these apostates as *"wild waves of the sea, casting up their own shame like foam."* If you've ever been to the beach, you know that the ocean's waves continually splash up onto the shore. The very head of the wave usually turns frothy as it "breaks" onto the sand in preparation for rolling back out to sea.

The apostate is like that. They are normally uncontrolled and uncontrollable. Because they can often be loud or overpowering in personality, they come to the point where they do not care who sees what they do or how they act in front of others.

Most people do not like conflict. We like to avoid it if at all possible. Leaders in churches are given the responsibility of having to *deal* with true conflict and should not turn away from it. To do so may ultimately mean harm for that congregation. Leaders should not shirk their responsibility of protecting the flock.

The apostate reaches a point where he will flaunt his lifestyle to others, and he'll do so in a way that often pre-empts others from addressing the situation. Yet their shame is clearly seen if leaders will step back and simply look at the situation the apostate is creating. Once seen, it should not be avoided.

This is especially true when the leaders sense that the pastor they have hired is eventually seen as an apostate. If he is preaching a *form* of spiritual emptiness based on simple platitudes, he is not only doing nothing good for that church but is reducing the effectiveness of that church by not edifying the saints, which is his God-given role.

Many Emergent Churches are just like this as they have watered down the gospel to mean little more than being socially minded and aware of needs in society. Gone is the belief that salvation is available only through Jesus, replaced with an "all roads lead to God" mentality.

Any pastor or teacher who teaches this type of theology is anathema to God and should not be given any time at all. The leaders within a church who are afraid to deal with an apostate pastor or teacher will reap nothing but the eventual destruction of that local congregation.

Ultimately, apostates – if in pastoral positions – want to change the fabric of that particular congregation through their liberal agenda. They may do this slowly over time, but that is their end goal.

Years ago, when I attended Philadelphia College of Bible, Tony Campolo was a well-known teacher and speaker (and still is in some circles). At the time, there was little that caused red flags with respect to his teaching.

Now, however, it is very easy to see that Tony Campolo does not represent the truth of Jesus. He does not teach the same gospel that Jesus taught, or Peter, or Paul, or anyone else who wrote part of the New Testament. He preaches a socialized, liberal gospel that actually winds up keeping people *from* receiving Jesus because there is not necessarily a need for them to do so. There are many people like this, and Jesus warned that as the end approached, we would see an increase in apostates and those who claim to be the Messiah.

When I read books or articles by Campolo, or Rick Warren, Brian McLaren, Tony James, or some other leader within the Emergent or Postmodern Church movement, it is easy to see their shame as foam. When you stand on the shore and the next wave comes in, it rushes toward you with the foamy water enveloping your feet and possibly higher, depending upon how far up the shore it travels before it breaks.

As you stand there, you see and experience the power of the water just off shore. When you wade out into that water, it literally picks you up and moves you where it goes.

On the shore, this same wave has little to no power to move you at all. It simply rushes around your feet and splashes, but there you stand, feet firmly placed in sand. While you might sink in the wet sand a bit, that little wave and foam that was once a mighty wave, taller than you are, does nothing except wash up around your feet.

The apostate *seems* to have power. In fact, people are attracted to people like this because they seem to possess something that you don't have and it attracts you, so you move closer. Soon, if you are not careful, you are under their spell.

If you are eventually given the grace to see their shallowness, you come to recognize that what you once thought was power was simply boisterousness and impiety. In fact, they may now appear to you to be just as they are – *obnoxious* liars – and you wonder why you did not see that before.

Apostates present themselves as one thing but are quite the opposite. Whether Tony Campolo realizes it or not, he is preaching another gospel, and as Paul says, "*let him be accursed!*" (cf. Galatians 1:8-9). This is the apostate.

Jude's final description in this section of his letter refers to stars of the sky. He says these apostates are like "*wandering stars, for whom the black darkness has been reserved forever.*"

A wandering star probably refers to a shooting star that has no solid trajectory, and while it may appear bright in the sky for a few seconds (or less), it is gone and forgotten immediately afterwards. Like this star, apostates arrive with promises of spiritual growth and fulfillment, but offer little in the way of actually fulfilling those promises. They are proverbial flashes in the pan. Though they may be here today and gone tomorrow, the damage they cause can last for a long time.

With all of these references and metaphors, it appears that Jude really wants his readers to understand what he is saying and to grasp the importance of it. Apostates are no good at all. They bring nothing of eternal value and they leave only destruction in their wake.

Think of Jim Jones. He started out on fire and gathered many people to him. How did the whole Jim Jones debacle end? It ended with 900 men, women, and children dead in a mass suicide from cyanide-laced Kool-Aid in the jungles of Guyana. How could that happen, we wonder? It happens because of the fleshly power of the apostate and the lack of biblical knowledge by the average church-goer today.

How about David Koresh? He and his followers burned to death in his Texas compound after a fire began when the ATF flooded into the compound to take him down.

These are just two examples of how badly things can go. Thankfully, not all situations end like this, but the damage that apostates can do, whether they are pastors, teachers, or simply members of a congregation, can be devastating, and at all costs leaders should always be on the look-out for these wolves. Just as the shepherd is always watchful for the real wolf in the wild who comes at night to stalk the sheep, so should the leaders in a church be constantly aware of the fact that someone, somewhere, is out there, and they will do what they can to advance their own position, leaving problems and broken relationships in their wake. The church must guard against this onslaught.

Chapter 7

Enoch's Warning

"It was also about these men that Enoch, in the seventh generation from Adam, prophesied, saying, "Behold, the Lord came with many thousands of His holy ones, to execute judgment upon all, and to convict all the ungodly of all their ungodly deeds which they have done in an ungodly way, and of all the harsh things which ungodly sinners have spoken against Him." Jude 1:14-15

If you take the time to read *The Book of Enoch*, you will read about his warning of the judgment that is coming at the end of the age, which I believe to be this current age in which we are living. Remember, there are two ages, as far as the Jewish sages were concerned: this age and the one to come. The age to come is considered to be the age of the Messiah.

Enoch lived during a time of unprecedented evil, yet he himself was *not* evil and walked with God (cf. Genesis 5:22). God considered Enoch to be righteous and in fact took him to heaven while he was still alive.

Because of the tremendous amount of evil that existed during his time, Enoch also knew that things would become far *worse*, due to the visions God gave him. Yet it was the same *type* of evil, just on a much grander scale than in his age.

Ultimately, evil is caused by ungodly people who give into their evil desires, and we know this. These people are perfectly described by Paul in the first chapter of Romans.

"For the wrath of God is revealed from heaven against all ungodliness and unrighteousness of men who suppress the truth in unrighteousness, because that which is known about God is evident within them; for God made it evident to them" (Romans 1:18-19).

This is almost exactly what Enoch says (quoted by Jude), but of course, using different terminology. In both Paul's and Enoch's words, we understand that evil is caused by ungodly or unrighteous people who *suppress the truth* with their unrighteous lives. They want so much to be free of any concept of a holy God that they not only live the way they want to live, deliberately doing what they *know* is wrong, but they also encourage others to do the same because it validates their own lives. The more who follow their example, the greater the chance of society forgetting about God altogether.

As I write this, riots are raging in the United Kingdom. Burning, looting, and destruction are ongoing, and the police seem helpless to stop it. More than one person has justified the rioting by saying that this shows the rich that they (the rioters and poor) can do what they want to do. Great reasoning, isn't it? *"Professing themselves wise..."*

That type of "reasoning" is insane. It was the same thing when Los Angeles broke out into riots a number of years ago over the verdict related to the Rodney King situation. The people who rioted and burned buildings wound up rioting, burning, and looting in their own neighborhoods, destroying businesses of people who often lived among them. It was absolutely ridiculous, and once a mob mentality takes over, all logic goes out the window.

It is this type of godlessness that will ultimately bring our Lord back in judgment to this earth. It will come at the end of the Tribulation period of seven years, and it will arrive just as the Antichrist has mustered all his troops in his attempt to keep Jesus from stepping foot on this planet.

Revelation 5 shows us that the Lamb who was worthy to take the seven-sealed scroll was Jesus, and the seven-sealed scroll is the earth's title deed. The judgments that pour forth from that document once it is opened do so because Jesus was found worthy to open it.

It is interesting that Jesus was found worthy to open a book or scroll that contained terrible judgments that are to be poured out over the earth and all who live here. This is proof that at the cross, Jesus defeated the powers of darkness and regained the title deed to the earth, which Satan stole by successfully tempting Adam and Eve to sin through rebellion.

Note when Jesus was being tempted by Satan in Matthew 4, Satan offered Him all the kingdoms of the world because Satan controlled them and they were in his power to do what he wanted with them. Jesus did not argue the point because He knew it was true. Jesus simply rejected the offer outright because He knew that He would eventually regain the title deed to earth by taking the hard road, the way of the cross, whereas Satan was tempting Jesus to *circumvent* the hard way.

It was the cross work of Jesus that regained for Him the title deed to the earth. In Revelation 5, Jesus is found worthy to open that deed and *give* it to the Father. The ability of Jesus here to *give* the title deed to earth back to the Father is proof that this earth (at that future point) no longer belongs to Satan.

The reason that Jesus needs to physically reign from His father David's throne in Jerusalem at some future point is to actually *prove* possession of the earth. The Antichrist wants to keep this from happening, so for the entire second half of the Tribulation he works to gain control of the world so that he can muster the world's forces in a last-ditch attempt to keep Jesus' feet from touching the earth.

Once Jesus physically comes to earth, the entire universe will see the proof that He owns this earth once again. He will then judge those on the earth and will reign for 1,000 years in Jerusalem. This does not mean he is not ruling now. It simply means that God – being legally-minded – will fulfill the Law that relates to His physical reign, just as He has fulfilled other aspects of the prophecies related to His birth, life, death, and resurrection. Not one jot or tittle will go unfulfilled.

When Jesus returns, He will vanquish evil, sequestering Satan to the Bottomless Pit for 1,000 years and dealing with any problems that come up during His reign immediately and with a rod of iron (cf. Psalm 2:9; Revelation 2:27). The entire swelling of evil will result in its final expulsion when Jesus judges all things. Of course, the final judgment – the Great White Throne Judgment – will occur at the end of His millennial reign (cf. Revelation 20:11-15).

All evil, ungodliness, and unrighteousness ultimately and inevitably lead to one place: *judgment*. It is because of all evil that this judgment is coming. Apostates help bring that judgment because they live ungodly and unrighteous lives, due simply to the fact that they themselves are ungodly and unrighteous and can do nothing else.

Notice the triple threat, so to speak. Jude calls these individuals ungodly because they have been participating in ungodly *deeds*, done in an ungodly *way*, and with ungodly *speech*. There is nothing good in them, three times evil. Evil completely permeates their lives because it has affected their way of life, the things they do, and the things they say. Evil and ungodliness cannot be separated from apostates because it is how they are composed.

Jude tags onto this the idea that the reality of the apostate's character can be seen in their *attitudes*. *"These are grumblers, finding fault, following after their own lusts; they speak arrogantly, flattering people for the sake of gaining an advantage."*

Notice first of all that apostates are ultimately *grumblers*. They like to complain for a number of reasons. First, it upsets the established order and tends to confuse people, throwing them off balance a bit. Second, it can also work to make these apostates *seem* more intelligent than others because they are seeing something that nobody else has noticed.

People generally like to surround themselves with people who are intelligent. It is the insecure person who finds people who are not of their own status because that makes them look better.

An apostate who complains about something in the church may ultimately be seen as a type of prophet, dutifully warning those in the church about some potential danger. In truth, the apostate is doing what he can to create factions, which will force people to take *sides*. Once those sides are created, the fabric of that church begins to fail, and it is not long before that church splits into two different bodies.

People who like to cause problems can sound charming or even act "hurt" when they do it. They try to give the impression that they're simply speaking out for the good of the body, when in truth, their design and plan is to oust someone and elevate themselves. Much of this is done surreptitiously at first until the apostate has enough numbers behind him to bring his concerns out into the open.

We've probably all heard of situations where part of the church body got together against the pastor because of the complaints of one or two people. Had the apostate been completely honest, he would have taken his concerns to the pastor and the pastor only. The fact that people do not follow biblical procedure immediately shows that they are not interested in doing things God's way, but *their* way.

You'll also notice in Jude's very picturesque language that not only do these apostates grumble and find fault, but they do so to follow after their own lusts. They have wants and they want those desires fulfilled. To make it happen, they carefully sow seeds of discontent and doubt. This causes people to cater to the apostate's own lusts. They couldn't care less about the good of the local body. They do not want the body to live in peace. They want their way and they will work to obtain it any way they can.

Jude also describes how they talk and why they speak as they do. He says *"they speak arrogantly, flattering people for the sake of gaining an advantage."*

Have you ever been on the receiving end of someone's flattery? Depending upon the situation, it can feel weird at times. If we have discernment and if the person doing the flattering has ulterior motives (which they often do), we may wind up seeing right through their empty compliments to realize that they are simply using flattering language to get their way.

People use all sorts of ways to get other people to do things for them. Guilt cues are common and flattery is another way people manipulate other people. In both cases, the person is trying to get someone to do something for *them* so that they will have their wants met.

Flattery is different from simply giving someone a compliment. Flattery can be described as *insincere praise*.[1] Most of us realize when this is being done. Someone who simply says "*Oh, your hair looks lovely*" or "*That suits looks very nice on you*" or something similar isn't necessarily trying to flatter us. Flattery is like the person who is the "yes" man or woman to their boss. Celebrities in Hollywood are often surrounded by people who constantly say "yes" to their every whim. A smart director will be free with the flattery with respect to the stars of his or her movie because it helps keep the star comfortable and at ease. If the star is at ease, the production shoot goes off much better.

Apostates don't use flattery on just anyone, though. They normally choose the weaker person in the crowd, the one who is not as secure and may have much insecurity. All of a sudden, here is this charming person paying attention to the insecure person, covering them with flattery. It's not long before that person becomes putty in the hands of the apostate.

All of this can bring about the type of changes that the apostate wants and needs. If the apostate doesn't like the pastor because he constantly preaches the truth, that same apostate may start working deep in the shadows to bring about the change he needs to see.

We attended one church in which this situation existed. A certain individual always remained the background and got other people to do his dirty work by getting them involved and worked up over concerns *he* had. Because of the *other* individual's personality, he would take off on his own and do exactly what the first individual wanted done, investing his own energy into the situation, doing the bidding of the person who wished to remain in the background.

---

[1] http://dictionary.reference.com/browse/flattery

The leaders in that church, though they "talked" to that man on numerous occasions, never went to the extreme of putting him out of the church even for a short time. He was a tither and his entire family was involved in church work. With him gone, the family would of course follow, which would leave a tremendous hole both financially and physically and which would be extremely difficult to fill.

Notice that Jude finishes off this section by stating that all of the ungodliness of the apostates is ultimately directed at God Himself. This makes sense if you stop to consider it, since all forms of evil are directed at God in the end. Though the apostate deals with people and manipulates them to get what he wants, ultimately, the apostate is attacking God, even if that apostate is immediately and indirectly attacking the pastor or some other person in that church.

When the apostate involves himself in gossip, or adopts a malevolent attitude toward someone, or complains so that others are worked up into a tizzy, major changes will occur in the local congregation of any church. However, God in Jesus is the Builder of that Church, so any attack on it is an attack on Him.

This is Jude's point. The apostate not only harms the local body, but since God takes it personally, He and He alone will be the ultimate vengeance on that situation because it is His Name that is at stake.

All ungodliness attacks God's character. God has promised to deal with it at the end of the age. Enoch warned of it, and Jude reminds us of it.

Chapter 8

Mockers in the Last Day

"But you, beloved, ought to remember the words that were spoken beforehand by the apostles of our Lord Jesus Christ, that they were saying to you, 'In the last time there will be mockers, following after their own ungodly lusts.' These are the ones who cause divisions, worldly-minded, devoid of the Spirit." Jude 1:17-19

To mock something literally means to ridicule it or make fun of it. Jude warns his readers that they should "remember," which implies they have been told at least once before about what he is going to remind them.

We know that Paul talked about this same situation in 2 Timothy 3:1-5 when he detailed the difficulties that would exist in the End Times. My book titled *"SELF"* goes into great detail about this, and I also have an audio series on this same subject, which can be heard at *OnePlace.com/ministries/study-grow-know.*

Peter as well references this problem in 2 Peter 2:1-3: *"But false prophets also arose among the people, just as there will also be false teachers among you, who will secretly introduce destructive heresies, even denying the Master who bought them, bringing swift destruction upon themselves. Many will follow their sensuality, and because of them the way of the truth will be maligned; and in their greed they will exploit you with false words; their judgment from long ago is not idle, and their destruction is not asleep."*

In fact, if you take the time to read through 2 Peter 2, you will read a good deal of verbiage similar to that of Jude as Peter describes these false prophets who parade their arrogance and take advantage of the average person. All of this was for their own ends.

"Daring, self-willed, they do not tremble when they revile angelic majesties, whereas angels who are greater in might and power do not bring a reviling judgment against them before the Lord. But these, like unreasoning animals, born as creatures of instinct to be captured and killed, reviling where they have no knowledge, will in the destruction of those creatures also be destroyed, suffering wrong as the wages of doing wrong. They count it a pleasure to revel in the daytime. They are stains and blemishes, reveling in their deceptions, as they carouse with you, having eyes full of adultery that never cease from sin, enticing unstable souls, having a heart trained in greed, accursed children; forsaking the right way, they have gone astray, having followed the way of Balaam, the son of Beor, who loved the wages of unrighteousness; but he received a rebuke for his own transgression, for a mute donkey, speaking with a voice of a man, restrained the madness of the prophet." (2 Peter 2:10-16)

In the above text, Peter uses similar phrases and lines of reasoning as does Jude. Speaking of individuals who are apostates, Peter says they are *daring* and *self-willed*. These people do what they want to do because they are their highest authorities. They refuse to answer to anyone else. They will put up resistance when people try to point out their error and will likely turn the tables so that the person addressing them will be seen as the problem child, not them.

These same individuals are daring because they really have no clue what they are truly up against. If they understood the powers they tried to oppose, they would turn to jelly. Instead, because of their lack of understanding, they move ahead without concern. They have no fear ("do not tremble") because they are really clueless. They speak against angels, and when nothing happens to them, they grow more empowered.

I love how Peter calls these men *"stains and blemishes."* That's exactly what they are, but of course they do not see it that way, and too many people in the local congregations do not see it that way either because they are attracted to such individuals.

I've already mentioned people like Tony Campolo, Rick Warren, and a few others. While it's not my intent to necessarily single people out, since these individuals are so well-known and have such huge followings, it is good to use them as an example of people who do not teach the truth, yet are held in high esteem in spite of it.

However, as far as the Lord is concerned, because they preach another gospel (though they would vehemently disagree), they are nothing but stains and blemishes. They actually take delight in the way they have deceived people. I doubt seriously if some of the leaders we know of today truly believe that they are themselves deceived or that they are deceiving people. I have my doubts about them. In fairness, some may simply be completely misinformed where the fundamentals of the faith are concerned. The result is the same, though.

In Rick Warren's case, his background is one in which he was mentored by Robert Schuller. Schuller's theology is hardly orthodox, and it is understandable that Warren's would not be either.

People like Warren may honestly believe what they preach is the truth, but the real truth will come out and they will one day be made aware of their error. Hopefully for them, it will be on *this* side of eternity where they have a chance to repent, rather than when they stand before the Lord after their death, when all chances for repentance are gone forever.

Recently, Rick Warren held some type of global peace conference, in which he had Dr. Oz (from TV) as one of the main speakers. Dr. Oz, though not Arab, is a devout Muslim. Others also shared the platform with Warren and Oz to bring together many voices representing differing religious perspectives into one voice. In beginning his conference, Warren actually took the time to apologize to members of the Islamic faith for the way they have been treated.

Rick Warren seems to be out to create a kingdom for himself. He wants to be all things to all people. I'm sure he would not like that description of mine, but the truth seems to be that he is doing whatever he can to help achieve world peace through his many programs and conferences. The Bible says that while we should live at peace with one another as far as we are able to do so, we should not expect true peace until the Prince of Peace returns. Yet too many today act and live as if Jesus did not say or teach anything like that.

Today, Preterism, Reformed and Covenant Theology is on the rise. In general – though there are exceptions – these individuals believe that Jesus "returned" spiritually in A.D. 70 with the destruction of Jerusalem and the Temple by the Roman armies under Titus. Though they believe that Jesus' return was one of a spiritual nature, this is in direct opposition to Jesus' own words in the Olivet Discourse as well as the words of the angels in Acts 1, when they indicated that the same way Jesus *left* this earth, He will *return*. He left physically, and will return the same way. Many apparently disagree with Jesus on this very clear reality.

Today, if you believe in the *physical* return of Jesus one day, expect to be laughed at or ridiculed. Now, it is no surprise, of course, that the world will ridicule Christians for such a belief. However, it is a bit frustrating to say the least when individuals within Christendom join in that ridicule.

It doesn't help when people like Harold Camping predict that the Lord is going to return May 21, 2011, and when that doesn't pan out, change it to the Lord returned "spiritually" at that time. This gives the world greater reason to laugh and increase the mockery towards Christians.

Yet this is what is happening today. Most leaders within the Emergent or Postmodern Church also mock the idea that Jesus is going to return. They believe, rather, that as Christians work to create a better society, Jesus will gain more of a foothold over the entire earth and the earth will slowly, consistently become more of what it was meant to be.

This type of thinking is insane in light of the conditions in the current world system. We have seen countries collapse and need bailing out by the European Union (EU) and we have experienced the many unprecedented deaths and destruction caused both by man and because of the many natural disasters.

Moreover, the hateful rhetoric continues to spew surrounding the situation in the Middle East, with no plausible end in sight. The world to a great degree now stands opposed to Israel like never before in recent history.

People are becoming exactly as Jesus, Paul, Peter, and Jude described for us, yet millions don't see it, and too many of these people are in the churches. They dutifully hold to their wishful thinking that one day the church will have such an effect on the world that it will become much better, as if wishing for it will make it so. This is in spite of what God says about what He is doing now and what He will do then in the end.

According to the Bible, this world will not get better by itself, any more than Evolution is fact. We are seeing more greed, more avarice, more hatred, more war, skirmishes, and rumors of war throughout the globe than ever before. The world is *not* getting better. It is getting far worse, just as the Bible predicted.

When they aren't mocking those of us who believe that Jesus is going to physically return to this earth one day, they are accusing us of *wanting* the world to get worse. One radio show host and well-known figure within Preterism accused me of *wanting* the Tribulation to happen so it would destroy the Jews; therefore, he accused me of being anti-Semitic! What nonsense. First of all, I do not *want* the Tribulation to occur, but I believe the Bible teaches that it *will* occur. Second, I do not want the Jews to be extinguished, and even though the Tribulation will be horrific and multitudes will die, including Jews, God will reserve for Himself a Remnant. This final Remnant will be the ones who – as a nation – will inherit the full scope of Land that God originally set aside for the Israeli nation.

Mocking is generally done when the individual has no serious answer or rebuttal to something. Sarcasm or ridicule is used in place of a solid response. Unfortunately, I have been guilty of this myself. While sarcasm has its place, as a rule, it should not be used as a regular form of rejoinder or rebuttal because it accomplishes nothing and does not further the conversation.

When I am mocked or scorned because of my personal belief that the Bible teaches that Jesus will return one day to set up His Millennial Kingdom from which He will reign from David's throne in Jerusalem, I cannot take it personally. I have to merely understand from Scripture that this is going to be the norm for these times because God is not only giving people over to themselves, but is sending a strong delusion so that they will believe the lie (cf. 2 Thessalonians 2:11). This is simply the way things will be, and I had better prepare myself for it, or I will be overcome by it.

Again, Jude is taking the time to remind his readers that in the end, mockers will come, and they will simply scorn everything that authentic believers hold dear, as taught in Scripture. The reason these individuals do this is because they are following their own lusts. They want no part of God. They want to do what they want to do and live their life their way without having to feel as though they answer to anyone other than themselves.

These people ridicule because the truth gets in the way of fulfilling their lusts. They will often become angry at people like me who deign to believe that when Jesus said upon His return every eye will see Him (cf. Matthew 24), this is exactly what will happen. I believe that His return is going to be seen like lightning flashing from one end of the sky to the other. It is going to be a purposeful return and no one will miss it. This is what Jesus said, so to not believe that is to call Him a liar. How can I do that when I know that He is not a liar? In Him, there is nothing but truth.

Mockers believe that the idea of Jesus returning physically some day is what myths and fantasies are made of, and by believing this we are ignoring our own responsibility to help make life on this planet a better place. Ultimately, mockers believe that things like environmental groups and peace groups are what will, in the final analysis, bring this world to the point where God wants it to be. This is bunk, in my opinion.

God has given us His *plan*. He has told us beforehand, and we have a choice to believe that or to disbelieve it. For mockers, the truth bothers them because it intrudes on their particular plans and world view. They don't want people preoccupied with something as fanciful as Jesus' Second Coming. They want people to focus on *them* so that they will get done what they want done. This is the apostate.

Those who mock do so because they themselves do not understand the fundamental truths of Christianity. Jesus said He would return physically. The angels in Acts 1 said He would return physically. What more do we need?

Because of the technology we have today, it is difficult for some to imagine Jesus parting the sky and breaking through it. These same individuals have a tough time imagining a time when there will be a final world dictator known as the Antichrist. Yet what we see all around us are signs that this is going to be the case.

Our world's economy is crumbling. The United States is heading towards financial disaster. In fact, we are on the very doorstep of financial ruin, and if we continue in this same direction for the next four years, we can be guaranteed to look back and see little left of this country. Russia's Putin has condemned the United States because the world depends upon the dollar and we have not been good stewards of it. China is angry with us for the same reason.

There is a good amount of vitriol against the U.S., and many countries throughout the world want some other currency so that they do not have to rely on the dollar as the world's economic standard. Besides economic upset, we are experiencing severe civil and social unrest throughout the world and in parts of the United States. It seems as though the fires are no sooner put out in one area than the world experiences another conflagration from another country or two.

In the meanwhile, the Islamic nations are pushing for Islam to dominate the world in more and more countries, and even areas in the United States are seemingly opening the door to Islam, catering to their "needs." A number of places in the U.S. have become literally overrun with Muslims who want Sharia law as their determining factor.

Islam looks forward to a Final Mahdi, who it is said will usher in world peace. This is exactly what Christians look for, but those of us who know the order of events will not be fooled by the Final Mahdi if we are here to see him when he rises. Jews will, though, at least at first, and Daniel 9:24-27 is clear that this same leader will turn against the Jewish nation three and a half years after he has brokered a covenant with them with the surrounding nations.

The Bible was written by God thousands of years ago. In fact, he took roughly 40 human authors over a period of approximately 1,600 years and created His testimony to the world. He told us way ahead of time so that there is no excuse. Yet we have people who have come along with their own interpretations of God's Word so that what God *said* and originally *meant* bears little to no resemblance to what is often taught today.

These people are mockers, changing the meaning of God's holy Word for their own purposes. They are unafraid of the ramifications. They want to see things happen their way, and they want to attract people to them who will come under their spell. They use flattery to gain the advantage just as Jude says, and they couldn't care less how they distort God's Word as long as they gain what they set out to achieve.

As time continues to progress, more mockers will come to the fore, and the attacks will become more vicious against those who take God's literal meaning from His Word (that's *literal*, not *literalistic*). These people are chasing after their own lusts because they are worldly-minded. They want what the world has to offer. Whether they want lots of money, expensive cars, large homes, extravagant vacations, or all the rest, they chase after it because it is something they want to have. They have no time for God's Word because as

Jude says, they are *devoid* of the Spirit. He is, of course, referring to the Holy Spirit.

The people who are without the Holy Spirit have no spiritual discernment whatsoever, yet they can project a spirit of discernment because they are great actors. People fall into the holes they create because they seem to have an air of authority, and the people hearing them have not personally studied God's Word themselves, so they do not know the difference. Because of this, they don't know the first thing about His teachings.

Folks like these are easily manipulated by people from cults because they have no biblical knowledge of their own and therefore no spiritual discernment to uphold them when they are confronted by members of cults or apostates. In the end, these mockers are the exact opposite of authentic believers. They have no Spirit, they are worldly-minded, and they are literally bereft of God's power since they do not belong to him.

There are too many people like this doing whatever they can to worm their way into local congregations and take advantage of the people there. Remember, they do this because they want to use people to fulfill their own personal needs and wants.

As Jude says, because of the nature of these apostates, who mock what they do not understand and do what they can to puff themselves up, they wind up creating disagreements, and eventually divisions in local bodies will occur. They cause people to take sides over many things that do not matter, though certainly some things do matter.

The objective seems to be for these apostates to keep the local congregation in a state of flux, because in doing so, the congregants are off balance and can be swayed one way or another. They are not interested in a peaceful, local body of believers where love is the rule. In such an environment, they cannot accomplish anything.

Whether they do it intentionally or whether it simply happens because of their presence, divisions are a hallmark of their involvement in a local body. Apostates thrive in such an environment. They love it and they love to keep changing things up.

Apostates as pastors will do this as well, because again, it keeps people off balance. If people are off balance, they can be moved one way or another. If they are solid in their relationships with one another and the Lord, it is difficult to move them.

One day, apostates who mock will be gone – *permanently*. Until then, authentic believers need to simply hold onto His Word and the truth found within. God's Word is true. What He says, He will do. It is as simple as that.

Mockers and apostates do what they can to make His Word more difficult and convoluted. In this way, people come to depend upon the teaching of the apostate because they don't want to trust their own judgment, and they certainly don't want to lean on the Holy Spirit for spiritual education and edification. However, this is exactly what we *are* to do if we are to avoid being another victim of the ever-present apostate.

Chapter 9

Keep Yourselves

"But you, beloved, building yourselves up on your most holy faith, praying in the Holy Spirit, keep yourselves in the love of God, waiting anxiously for the mercy of our Lord Jesus Christ to eternal life." Jude 1:20-21

The sense of Jude's words here is that authentic believers are not at all like apostates, and because of that, should make sure that they do not begin to *act* like them. In our insecurities, we have a tendency to fear what we don't understand, or fear the change that an apostate may be trying to foist upon a group.

Instead of fearing, we should go to the Lord in prayer. Jude says we should pray in the Holy Spirit. I don't believe he is telling people to pray in tongues as some tend to think. I believe Jude is speaking of our prayer time when we communicate with the Father through the empowering of the Holy Spirit. The most important thing a Christian can do is to pray unceasingly for God's will to be accomplished.

The pattern for this type of prayer is found in the Garden of Gethsemane when Jesus prayed what He wanted to occur but quickly *affirmed* the Father's will. In other words, Jesus prayed, *"not mine, but thy will be done"* (cf. Mark 14:36; Luke 22:42; see also John 6:38). This should be the hallmark of the Christian's life, wanting nothing but God's will to be accomplished.

We see in the Garden of Gethsemane how difficult this was for our Lord, with Luke describing blood flowing from Jesus' brow because of the tremendous pressure of the situation. Jesus saw what was ahead of Him, with the pain, the torture, and the thirst. Most of all, He saw the fact that the Father would have to turn His back on His own Son because He would need to pour out wrath on Jesus, since Jesus had literally become sin for us. Paul tells us this when he states, *"He made Him who knew no sin to be sin on our behalf, so that we might become the righteousness of God in Him"* (2 Corinthians 5:21).

Jesus, who was without even the *hint* of sin, *became* sin – was *seen as if He had sinned* – and because of this, became our propitiation. God poured out His wrath on Jesus instead of pouring it out on us. Jesus willingly succumbed to that fate because it was the reason He came in the first place.

Jesus prayed all the time that He would only perform the Father's will. He did this in the power of the Holy Spirit. This is what we are to do. Jude is not talking about some ecstatic prayer language but an overwhelming desire to do only that which the Father wants us to do. This can only be accomplished through prayer, which is seeking the Lord's face, that His will would be our food.

Jude tells us that if this was how Jesus did it, how much more do we need to follow His example? This is what builds us up in our mutual holy faith. As we pray for His will only, we wind up submitting ourselves to Him for that purpose. Instead of wanting our own desires filled (like the apostate), we learn to give up our wants in exchange for *His* will in *our* life.

Whether we understand His will at the time is not the point. By trusting Him that what happens in our life is His will, our *faith* will be strengthened and therefore will *increase*. That increase in faith will build us up *spiritually*.

Interestingly enough, Jude tells us to keep ourselves in the love of God. This does not mean that we can lose our salvation. It means that we should – through prayer – come to Him for everything. As we spend time praying for His will, not only will our faith increase as we see Him accomplish things in our life, but our love for Him will grow as well. One works off the other.

In 2009, my family and I experienced something that was very difficult for us, and we entered onto a path that seemed like the correct path. However, at every turn, we were buffeted. We felt as if there was a wall against us.

It wasn't until two years later that we realized why we had experienced all the frustration. God was getting us ready to move in a different direction, so He did not allow us to get comfortable in the previous path.

Looking back over the past two years, I can see exactly why things happened as they did. It's absolutely perfect! His timing is uncanny. However, remembering what things were like at the beginning, back in 2009, we really had little clue. We knew we should move in the situation so we did, but it was only later that we realized what it was all about.

As I look back, I can see that my faith has grown. Not only this, but my love for Him has grown as well. It would not be what it is now had He not taken us through the situation He took us through. It was that situation that brought about the growth that God intended for us, and I am glad for it. As I say, though, when we were going through it, it was difficult at best to see where we were going.

I'm sure you've had situations like this, and hopefully, as you look back at them, you realize what you have gained because of those situations. God is extremely good, and while we understand this fact *intellectually*, the only way we learn it *experientially* is when we submit ourselves to Him, trusting Him to accomplish what He sets out to do, whether the end is in sight or not.

Jude finishes up this section with the statement that we are waiting anxiously for the mercy of our Lord Jesus Christ to eternal life. This is a very heady truth. We are in the world, but not of the world. While here, we are to complete the will He has given us to complete.

Yet because we are in this world and can only vaguely "see" the coming eternity, we live by a faith that defies natural explanation. It is that faith that brings us closer to God as we exercise it, and as stated, our love for Him grows as well.

Living here tends to make us anxious. We become anxious over many things. We may be experiencing poor health, a recent death of a loved one, a job loss, or any number of things.

In this particular economy, life can hit us very hard financially. Financial worries can be extremely frustrating, and out of all our worries, these are among the most difficult to give to God, allowing Him to work things out.

My daughter recently experienced a situation at work where because of the uncertainty of her continued employ (she was not sure if the place she was working was going to remain open), she began looking for another job. She had worked at her current job for over six years and it was the first real job she had. Of course she was nervous and unsure. She looked around and found that there were a number of positions available for which she was qualified, and so she applied. She didn't know what to expect.

The Lord was far more gracious than He needed to be, because that evening, she received a call from one of the potential employers and scheduled an interview the next day. She went to the interview and they offered her a job that evening. The Lord did not have to do that, but He did, for her sake.

Since then her husband has received some good news at his work regarding his schedule and the chance of a promotion. The Lord does work things out, but He works them out according to His plan, not ours. This is what we need to be open to, and that only occurs when, as Jude said, we pray to Him in the power of the Spirit so that the only thing that occurs in our life is His will. Praying to Him like this provides us the grace to accept His will even when His will is not what we initially envisioned.

The more we pray to Him, empowered by the Holy Spirit, the more our faith is strengthened as we see His will unfold in our life. The more our faith is strengthened due to seeing His will accomplished in our lives, the more we come to love Him *for* that will. We come to recognize it as the only sustainable answer to our situation. He knows us inside and out. He knows what we need and He knows the best way to get us someplace. He knows all things, and the more we come to terms with that, the more we grow to love Him and let go of the things in this world that attempt to control us.

This is the exact opposite of how the apostate lives his life. While the apostate wants to control *other* people for his own edification, true believers want God to control all aspects of their life.

While the apostate responds only to his earthly lusts and wants others to follow suit, the authentic Christian hears and follows only

God's voice. This is the difference between the individual who truly loves God and the one who truly loves himself. On the outside, this may be at times difficult to discern, but over time, the apostate will be seen for what he is, just as the true Christian will be seen for what he is in Christ.

I think this is best summed up in Psalm 23.

> *"The LORD is my shepherd,*
> *I shall not want.*
> *He makes me lie down in green pastures;*
> *He leads me beside quiet waters.*
> *He restores my soul;*
> *He guides me in the paths of righteousness*
> *For His name's sake.*
> *Even though I walk through the valley of the shadow of death,*
> *I fear no evil, for You are with me;*
> *Your rod and Your staff, they comfort me.*
> *You prepare a table before me in the presence of my enemies;*
> *You have anointed my head with oil;*
> *My cup overflows.*
> *Surely goodness and lovingkindness will follow me all the days of my life,*
> *And I will dwell in the house of the LORD forever."*

The Lord *is* our Shepherd, and there is no one better to have in that position. He cares for us, and because He cares for us, we will never *want* for anything we truly need.

Even though we at times are surrounded by enemies, He creates a peaceful place in the midst of life's storms so that nothing touches us unless He allows. Note that though life can be thoroughly stressful at times, like the sheep led to the peaceful streams of life-giving water, so, too, does our Great Shepherd bring us to peaceful places within so that our soul is refreshed and restored. This comes from studying His Word in order to know more about Him.

The Psalm goes on to say that everything He does in our life, He does *for His Name's sake.* He wishes to glorify Himself, and we are privileged to have Him do this *in* and *through* us. We may not understand what is happening at the time, but whether we understand it or not, we should be able to trust Him in spite of our lack of understanding.

He will guide us, and even when we feel we are surrounded by evil, He offers His protection. Is there any protection that is greater? Because of it, we have no reason to fear.

Just as the shepherd uses the rod and staff to redirect a sheep in the direction it should go, so too does our Great Shepherd direct our steps. The crook in the rod is used to gently catch the sheep around the neck, not to injure it, and not so the shepherd will *yank* the sheep, but so that the sheep will be directed in the proper path.

The shepherd also has the option of using the end of his staff to nudge the sheep one way or the other, sometimes so subtly that the sheep is hardly aware of it. In essence, then, God will direct us according to His plan and according to what is good for us.

David finishes this Psalm with high praise to God for His faithfulness and the fact that David had more than he ever thought possible. He was literally rich in spiritual blessings and so are we, though we often fail to take the time to realize it.

Jude ends this section of text by directing our attention to our greatest spiritual blessing, *eternal salvation.* There is nothing greater and nothing so undeserved. Yet God in His love and faithfulness carried His plan of redemption through to fruition so that those of us destined for hell could be legally and ultimately redirected toward heaven.

Chapter 10

Have Mercy

"And have mercy on some, who are doubting; save others, snatching them out of the fire; and on some have mercy with fear, hating even the garment polluted by the flesh." Jude 1:22-23

Because we have been shown tremendously undeserved mercy, we should not hesitate to show that mercy to others. At the same time, we need to be careful, because we have come to understand what we have been saved *from*, and because of it we recognize the dangers of the flesh and the sin that results from it.

Jude tells us to show mercy to some who doubt. Rather than become angry with them or desire to attack them for what we may see as faithlessness, we should approach them in gentleness, understanding the situation. Because of our humanity and our fallen nature, it is at times difficult to continue to believe. People experience doubts of all kinds where God is concerned. Even Job, as righteous as he was, experienced numerous doubts about God and his relationship with Him.

It is not unusual for people to doubt, especially in difficult times: when we lose a loved one, when things simply don't go as we think they should, or when life simply hands us lemons. It is especially normal for new Christians to doubt God, simply because they often lack the wisdom and discernment to understand.

Folks who have been Christians for years can also succumb to periods of doubt, in spite of how mightily God may have worked in their life beforehand. John the Baptist is a good example of this. He paved the way, as the Scriptures foretold he would, for Jesus. Yet when it was time for John to be taken out of this world, he wondered if Jesus really *was* the Messiah, or should they expect another? Jesus responded *not* with anger or frustration, but with love and kindness (cf. Matthew 11:4-6). There are some who make a big deal because of John's obvious doubting here, but the man was *human*. He was facing death. He had a moment of unnerving doubt. Jesus responded to those who would report back to John in prison with these words: *"Go and report to John what you hear and see: the BLIND RECEIVE SIGHT and the lame walk, the lepers are cleansed and the deaf hear, the dead are raised up, and the POOR HAVE THE GOSPEL PREACHED TO THEM. And blessed is he who does not take offense at Me."*

Jesus could have come down on John, but He understood that John's doubts were human, and though not what Jesus wanted, His answer helped John *re-establish* faith in Jesus. Jesus responded to John in a very loving, understanding way. Because of it, He did more to help John than He would have if He had gotten angry with him, don't you think? In essence, Jesus showed mercy on John because of John's human frailties. Don't forget, John was about to be executed, and that may have also created some fear or trepidation. How many of us can look death straight in the eyes, even though we know what awaits us on the other side? Death is a sobering concept.

Aside from using mercy, Jude tells us that depending upon the circumstances we may need to address a situation as if we are approaching a fire. We need to be extremely careful so that we are not burned in the process of pulling someone else out of the fire.

Of course, the imagery here is trying to extricate someone from a house or car fire. As you approach the situation, the heat from the fire can push you back. It's daunting. However, it is possible to get in, get the person, and get out without getting singed or burned, depending upon the nature of the fire and how severe it is at the start.

Normally, saving someone from a fire requires extremely quick reflexes. It doesn't take long for a home to become completely engulfed in flames, and once that happens, forget about trying to rescue anyone. In the early stages of a fire, it is possible – with a good deal of speed – to get into the burning home and remove the victim before they burn to death or die of smoke inhalation.

There will be some situations we will encounter where people are on their deathbeds. This will be the last opportunity they have to respond to the Lord. Will they? It may have nothing to do with what we say, but everything to do with the way we pray.

I am always amazed whenever I think of the thief on the cross. I stand in awe of that section of Scripture because there we see both thieves who were simply hurling abuse at Jesus one moment, and the next moment, one of those very thieves was now standing in Jesus' corner, defending Him against the ridicule and cowardice of the other thief. We can read about this narrative in Luke 23.

My question is, what happened that caused the one thief to turn from his stupidity, blindness, and selfishness to all of a sudden want to *defend* Jesus? What changed? Well, obviously, the man's eyes were opened and he saw the truth. From that new vantage point, he was now able to see that he had been wrong.

After this realization takes hold, he turns to Jesus with an apology of sorts. Certainly, he had been humbled, and because of that he was able to approach Jesus with this new attitude. It was this new attitude that prompted him to ask if Jesus would simply *remember* him when He (Jesus) came into His Kingdom. Jesus responded that he (the thief) would be with Him in paradise that very day.

So what happened? I can only guess. It is likely that both thieves witnessed Jesus' scourging, and they also likely witnessed and heard the abuse He received as He walked toward the hill on which He would be crucified. They would have also seen that Jesus did not retaliate in any way to those who scourged, scorned, and mocked Him.

Once at the crucifixion site, they saw more harassment hurled His way, and they saw how the soldiers treated Him and His belongings. They also noticed that a sign was placed above His head just as they (the thieves) had signs above theirs. These signs were essentially placed to inform the public what the crime was for which the victim was being executed.

The sign over Jesus' head indicated that He was a King. In fact, it did *not* say that Jesus *said* He was the King of the Jews. It said simply "*The King of the Jews.*" Was it this sign, along with Jesus' demeanor, that allowed the eyes of the one thief to open wide? It could be. We don't know for sure. All we know is that this thief received salvation on his deathbed, mere hours before he passed from this life to the next. I think this is what Jude means here when he speaks of *snatching them out of the fire*.

But Jude also provides one more scenario when he says that we should save some out of fear, hating even the clothing polluted by fleshly living. By the way, when Jude refers to our "saving" anyone, he of course is *not* saying that *we* do the saving. At the most, we only introduce a person to the One who actually does the saving. It is only in that sense that we save anyone.

In this last scenario, we need to exercise great caution because if we are not careful, we ourselves could be dragged down into those areas that are born of the flesh and have trapped the person we are attempting to help. We need to be diligent to ensure that this does not happen to us.

Chapter 11
Jude's Doxology

"Now to Him who is able to keep you from stumbling, and to make you stand in the presence of His glory blameless with great joy, to the only God our Savior, through Jesus Christ our Lord, be glory, majesty, dominion and authority, before all time and now and forever. Amen." Jude 1:24-25

This last part of Jude's letter represents some of the most powerful words ever penned. Many pastors have and continue to use this as the closing part of their service on Sundays. Here, we read fifty-one words that explain in a nutshell the blessing of salvation and our union with Jesus.

Jude asserts that Jesus is able to keep us from *stumbling*. Of course, Jude means that Jesus can keep us from *sinning*. This happens when *we* rely on Him, not when we rely on our own strength, such as it is.

If we faithfully approach Him during times that are difficult, when we are facing temptations to sin, and when we are experiencing frustration with life, He will strengthen us so that in spite of our circumstances, we will not succumb to temptation and commit sin. Jesus is more than capable of keeping us from stumbling. Are we willing to submit to His care so that He *will* keep us from stumbling?

Jude also tells us that this very same Jesus is quite capable of making us stand in His glorious presence with great joy. Consider that situation. Most people who believe that some type of god exists have fears about this god. Even Christians wonder if they will be afraid when they stand before God to give an account of our lives.

Jude is not only saying that we will *not* be afraid, but that we will experience incredible *joy*. This joy will rock us to our toes, as it were, because it will engulf our entire being.

Happiness is a bit superficial. You can be happy one moment and not happy the next. That's because happiness is often reliant upon *circumstances* that come into our life.

Consider this scenario: we are going along fine and happy about the fact that we will be heading to Disneyland this weekend with the family. As the time approaches, something goes severely wrong with the car and the money that was going to be used to enjoy Disneyland now needs to be spent on car repairs. Happiness goes out the window, replaced with sadness and frustration.

A person who is filled with joy will find a way to go around that frustration. The family is still here, so instead of going to Disneyland as originally planned, maybe a day at the local lake with a picnic will be great. Is Disneyland the source of joy or is health and family?

The reality is that when we stand before Jesus, there will be things that we will learn we did wrong in this life. However, the joy comes because we will *experience,* as we have never before experienced, what it means to be authentically saved. We will see how it works in the afterlife. Now, in this life, we base our understanding on God's Word, of course, but it's not truly as experiential as it will be after we die. Then, we will know and understand completely how Jesus' righteousness has been applied to our lives. Even though this is the case now, my resident sin nature continues to be at war with me, wanting me to do things that are opposed to God. It's a constant battle and works to diminish the joy within that comes from being saved. This will not be the case in the afterlife.

When I leave this life, I will also leave behind that sin nature, and the battle that I have lived with my entire earthly life will be over. I will then experience newness of life that I can only dream about now.

Why is it I will be able to stand in His glorious presence with great joy? It is because I will be *blameless* at that point. Right now, even though my sins – past, present, and future – are forgiven completely and Paul tells me in Ephesians 2 that I am now seated with Christ in the heavenly realm, I do not *feel* as though I am blameless because I still sin occasionally. Do I listen to my feelings or do I put my faith in God's Word? Well, hopefully, I trust in God's Word, in spite of the way I feel.

If Jesus is able to keep me from stumbling and to present me to Himself blameless, I will then, *because* of that, experience tremendous joy. It will be like no joy I have ever experienced in this life. Not my marriage, not the births of my daughter and son, not my daughter's marriage or anything else I experience here will give me the type of joy that I will experience there when I see Him, and I will know beyond all things that He loves me and sees me as righteous.

Even when I received salvation, though I was very excited, it will not compare with how I will understand it and experience it *there*, in the afterlife. Jude expresses what we will know and understand in the next life, and it is difficult for us to imagine now.

He then commits his readers "*to the only God our Savior, through Jesus Christ our Lord.*" This "*only God*" *is* Jesus Christ. Paul does this same thing, but says it just a bit differently in Titus 2:13: "*looking for the blessed hope and the appearing of the glory of* **our great God and Savior, Christ Jesus**." I've emphasized part of the text. Paul is not indicating *two* different individuals, as if God is one individual and Jesus is the other (though that is true in the triune sense). He is stating clearly that God *and* the Savior are one in the Person of Jesus Christ. Therefore, Jesus is God and Savior.

It is to Jesus that Jude directs his final comments. To Jesus "*be glory, majesty, dominion and authority, before all time and now and forever. Amen.*"

What Jude is saying is that Jesus existed *before all time*, He exists *now*, and He will continue to exist *forever*. Because of that, all glory, all majesty, dominion and authority is *His*. Jesus is God and is over all things. There is nothing above Him and all things are below Him, having been created *by* Him.

Jude's letter is short, but packed. It is brief, but alive with fullness. It is the furthest thing from being trite. It is a very profound document that in twenty-five verses outlines the *problem* of sin, the *path* of sin, and the ultimate *end* of sin.

Chapter 22
The End

Do you know *when* you will die? Are you aware of the *day* and *hour* when you will slip from this life into eternity? I'm betting you are not privy to that information. So why are you living as if you **do** *know when it will happen?* Putting a decision about Jesus off until another day is taking a huge chance because of the fact that you do not know when you will die. That is plainly simple, and logic alone demands that you do not put this decision off. Yet you do, because the thought of becoming a Christian makes you feel uncomfortable.

You wrongly believe that to become a Christian means that you have to change in a major way *before* Jesus will accept you. It means to you giving up the things you love now because if you love them, then obviously they are wrong and God does not love them.

You are putting the cart before the horse. You must understand that God is not rejecting you. He is not standing there, tapping His foot, demanding that you eliminate those things that He does not like before you can come to Him for salvation.

If you (or anyone) could do that, you would not *need* His salvation at all. It is because you and I do things that are not pleasing to Him that we need His salvation.

What do you do that you would like to no longer do? Do you drink excessively until you cannot control it? Do you play around with drugs? Do you eat too much food until you have become overweight, lethargic and sickly?

What other things are in your life that you do not like? Are you drawn to illicit extra-marital affairs? Do you have a problem with lust? Are you a shopaholic? Do you tend to tell lies a great deal because it makes you feel important, or to hide things about your life?

Do you find that you do not like people and you would prefer to be around animals or out in the woods than around people? Are you a workaholic? Do you place a high value on money and you find that you work very hard to obtain it?

Here's the problem. The enemy of our souls comes to us and tells us that God will never accept us until we get rid of those things. He lies to us that God essentially wants us "perfect" before He will be willing to meet us and grant us eternal life. This is completely untrue.

The other lie that our enemy tells us is that we should not become a Christian because the fun in our life will fly out the door. We will no longer be able to drink or do the fun things we enjoy now. We start to think that coming to God means becoming a doormat for people and having to fill our life with things we do not want to *ever* do.

These are all lies, and unfortunately, too many people believe them. First of all, God does not expect you to be "perfect" before you come to Him for salvation. If that were the case, no one would be able to ever approach Him.

Secondly, God does not say that He is going to take away all the things we enjoy and replace them with things we hate. What is wrong with enjoying the lake on your boat? What is wrong with spending a day with the family fishing or just relaxing in the mountains? There is nothing wrong with these things.

What God *will* do is begin to remove the things that have ensnared you so that life is actually draining from you, but you are not aware of it. For instance, maybe you drink excessively and you have tried everything you can think of to quit. You have gone to AA meetings, spent thousands of dollars on this program or that, and you have even used your own will power to free yourself from the addiction to alcohol, all to no avail.

The question is not: *do I need to quit before I come to Jesus*? The question is: *am I willing to allow Him to work in and through me to take away the addiction I have to alcohol*? Do you see the difference? Are you willing to allow Him to work in you to break that addiction so that you will become a healthier person, one who is able to think straight and one who learns to rely on Him for strength? That is all He wants you to be able to do. He knows you cannot break that addiction (or any addiction for that matter) with your own strength and willpower. Are you willing to allow Him to do it in and through you?

What if you are a workaholic? What if you have "things" like a boat, a house in Cancun, a large bank account, four cars, and more? Do you think that God is going to ask you to give it up, or worse, do you think that God will simply come in and take all of that from you? I know of nothing in Scripture that tells us He will do that.

What God will do with all of those who come to Him trusting Him for salvation is one thing, which begins the moment we receive salvation and will continue until the day we stand before Him. He will begin to create within us the character of Jesus (cf. Ephesians 2:10).

Here is a verse from the Old Testament that was said originally through the prophet Ezekiel to the people of Israel. While this was specifically stated to the Jews, it is applicable to all who receive salvation through Jesus Christ.

"I will give you a new heart and put a new spirit within you; I will take the heart of stone out of your flesh and give you a heart of flesh. I will put My Spirit within you and cause you to walk in My statutes, and you will keep My judgments and do them" (Ezekiel 36:26-27).

God is speaking here through Ezekiel, and He is saying that He will give the people a new heart of flesh, removing that old heart of stone. This is God's responsibility. God is the One who makes that happen. We are told in the book of Hebrews that God is the Author and Finisher of our faith (cf. Hebrews 12:2). This tells me that God is the One who changes me from within so that over time, my desires are slowly turned into His desires.

I recall years ago thinking that God wanted to do everything in my life that I did not want Him to do. I fell into the asinine belief that He wanted to change everything about me. What I learned is that yes, there are things that God does want to change about me. However, there is a lot that God originally gave me that He has also enhanced and used for His glory.

Maybe you are a workaholic who thinks that working hard is something God does not want you to do. This is not necessarily the case. He may have given you the ability and the knowledge to work in the area of finance for a great purpose. All He may wind up doing is dialing back your workaholic tendencies so that you have more time to enjoy your family and study His Word.

But you say you smoke, or drink, or use illegal drugs, and you don't want to give those up. As I stated, you can't give those up under your own power, and the fact that you have tried so many times has proven it to you.

But God knows what is and what is not good for you. Are you willing to *allow* Him to work in you to change your desires so that you no longer want to smoke, use illegal drugs, or drink nearly as much?

Then you say that you believe God wants to make you a Christian so you can become miserable. Isn't that what most Christians are – miserable? Not the Christians I know, and certainly not me, my wife, or our children.

Where does the Bible say that God wants us miserable? You will not find it. What God wants is for us to be blessed, and that begins when we receive salvation from His hand.

You know, if we would stop and take the time to consider the fact that this life is exceedingly short if we compare it to eternity, we will then realize that there is nothing so important that it should keep us from receiving Jesus as Savior and Lord.

Unfortunately, too many people do not consider the brevity of life. They think they will live forever, or at the very least, they will die when they are really old and gray. That will come too soon. Even though I have just recently turned 54, it still truly seems like yesterday that I was a young boy fishing in the Delaware River near Hobart, New York. There I spent many Saturdays fishing and simply enjoying being outdoors. How did life go by so very quickly? How could that have happened?

It has happened, and I am at a point in life where not only do I realize that this life is short, but I actually look forward to spending eternity with Jesus after this life. Does that sound morbid to you? It shouldn't, because by comparing this life to eternity, we should get a sense of what is truly important.

God does not expect us to become Mother Theresas. He does not necessarily expect us to give up everything and become missionaries in outer Mongolia. What God expects is for us to simply allow Him to change our character as He sees fit.

Over time, we may well find that we have simply stopped swearing without realizing it. Our desire for cigarettes or alcohol has nearly evaporated. Illicit affairs no longer enter the picture.

We also may find that some of the things we want to eliminate in our life become more pronounced. Often the enemy will do this to cause us to focus on something that God is not even doing in our lives at that point. It causes tension, frustration, and self-anger.

If you have gotten to this point in your life and you have not dealt with the question about Jesus, it is about time you do so. You need to stop what you are doing and realize a couple of things before you go through another minute in this life.

- **Sinner**: you need to realize that you are a sinner. You have sinned and you will continue to sin. Sin is breaking the laws that God has set up. We all sin. We have all broken God's laws and that breaks any connection we might have had with God.

Sin pushes us away from Him.

Romans 3:23 says, *"For all have sinned, and come short of the glory of God."* That means you and that means me. All means all. That is the first step. We need to recognize and agree with God that yes, we are sinners. I'm a sinner. You are a sinner. This results in God's anger, what the Bible terms "wrath."

- **God's Wrath**: Romans 1:18 says, *"For the wrath of God is revealed from heaven against all ungodliness and unrighteousness of men, who suppress the truth in unrighteousness."*

This is as much a fact as the truth that we are all sinners. Because we are sinners – by breaking God's law(s) – God has every right to be angry with us and ultimately destroy that which is sinful. If we choose to remain "in" our sinful states throughout this life, we will – unfortunately – be destroyed with the rest of sin.

Fortunately, there *is* a remedy, and it is salvation.

- **God's Gift**: In the sixteenth chapter of Acts, a jailer asks Paul this famous question: *what must I do to be saved?* The question was asked because Paul and Barnabas had been imprisoned, and while there, they began singing praises to God.

God then sent a powerful earthquake that opened the doors to all the prison cells, yet no one escaped. When the jailer arrived, he saw that everyone was still in their cells, and after seeing that miracle (what prisoner would not want to escape from prison?), turned and asked what he must do to be saved. He was speaking of the spiritual aspect of things. He wanted to know how he could be guaranteed eternal life.

The answer Paul gave the man was, *"Believe on the Lord Jesus Christ, and thou shalt be saved, and thy house"* (Acts 16:31).

This is not head knowledge or intellectual assent. This is *believing from the heart.* In fact, Paul makes a very similar statement in another book he wrote, Romans. He says, *"That if thou shalt confess with thy mouth the Lord Jesus, and shalt believe in thine heart that God hath raised him from the dead, thou shalt be saved. For with the heart man believeth unto righteousness; and with the mouth confession is made unto salvation"* (Romans 10:9-10).

When we fully believe something, we confess that it is true. It must begin in the heart because that is where the will is located. We must want to believe. We must endeavor to believe. We must seek to believe.

We must stop giving ourselves all the reasons to deny or ignore Jesus. As God, He became a Man, born of a virgin. He clothed Himself with humanity that He might show us how to live, and in so doing, would keep every portion of the law.

If Jesus was capable of keeping every portion of the law, then He would be found worthy to become a sacrifice for our sin – yours and mine. If He became a sacrifice for our sin, then all that we must do is embrace Him and His sacrificial death.

In short then, to become saved we must:

1. Admit (we sin)

2. Repent (want to turn away from it)
3. Believe (that Jesus is the answer)
4. Embrace (the truth about Jesus)

We **admit** that we are sinner, that we have sinned. This is nothing more than agreeing with God that we have broken His law. Can you honestly say that you have not broken God's law? If you admit to breaking even the "smallest" law, then you are a lawbreaker.

After we admit that we have sinned, the next step is found in **repenting**. Some believe that repenting is actually moving away from sin. This author believes that it is a willingness to move away from sin, and there is a difference.

As we have already discussed, it is impossible to stop sinning. Human beings simply cannot do it because as long as we live, we will have a sin nature, which is something within us that gives us a propensity to sin. As long as we have this inner propensity to sin or break God's laws, we will never be perfect in this life.

We cannot one day say, "Lord, I promise to stop sinning." If we do that, we are only kidding ourselves and setting ourselves up for major failure. We cannot stop sinning in this life. The most we can do is *want* to stop sinning and then spend the rest of our lives allowing God to create the character of Jesus within us, slowly, little by little.

Repenting is to decide that you no longer want to do the things that keep us out of heaven. We no longer wish to break God's laws. It is not promising God that we will never sin again.

Once we admit, then repent, we must **believe**. This is one of the most difficult things to do because believing that Jesus died in our place, that He lived a perfectly sinless life, is extremely difficult to believe. Our minds cannot grasp that truth. We must ask God to open our eyes to that truth so that we can embrace it.

While on the cross next to Jesus, the one thief joined the other thief in ridiculing Jesus. Then, all of a sudden – as we read in Luke 23 – this same thief that had just been ridiculing Him now turned to Him with a new understanding.

It was this new understanding that prompted the thief to say to Jesus, *"Lord, remember me when you come into your Kingdom."* Jesus looked at the man and responded to him, *"Today, you will be with me in paradise."*

What had occurred in the mind and heart of that thief from one moment to the next? One thing, and that one thing was that God opened the thief's eyes so that he could see the truth. It was as if the blinders fell off and he now saw and understood who Jesus was, even to the most cursory degree that Jesus was dying not for Himself, but for others.

It was this understanding, this awareness, which prompted the man to ask Jesus to simply be remembered. Jesus went way beyond it to promise the man that he would be with Jesus that day in paradise.

Please notice in Luke 23 that there is nothing in the chapter that tells us that the man promised Jesus he would give up sin, or that he would never sin again. There is nothing that tells us that thief took the time to enter into a final deathbed confession of his sins so that he could be absolved.

The thief made no promises to Jesus at all. What he experienced was the truth of who Jesus was and what Jesus accomplished for humanity. Jesus accomplished what we cannot. What is left is for each person to *admit*, *repent*, *believe*, and *embrace*.

Let me clarify here that though we do not see any verbal repentance from the thief, we know that he did repent. He admitted as well. How can we know this? Simply due to the thief's complete about-face with respect to his attitude toward Jesus. One minute, he was ridiculing Jesus, and the next, embracing Him. This is important. There is no way he could have or would have *embraced* Jesus had he not been humbled by the truth *about* Jesus.

Once the thief saw the truth, he was instantly humbled. Within himself, he knew that he was a sinner, and in fact the text states that this is what he told the other thief dying next to him. "*But the other answering rebuked him, saying, Dost not thou fear God, seeing thou art in the same condemnation? And we indeed justly; for we receive the due reward of our deeds: but this man hath done nothing amiss*" (Luke 23:40-41). Something happened within the heart of the one thief. In one moment, the thief went from harassing Jesus to recognizing his own sinfulness and then ultimately asking for grace, which was freely given to him.

Whether he said it or not, the thief went from haughtiness to humility in a very short space of time, and it was all because he saw the truth about Jesus. That truth helped him realize that he deserved his death and what would happen to him after death. He understood that Jesus did not deserve death.

From here, the thief fully embraced the truth about Jesus and was rewarded with eternal life because of it. He did not come off the cross to be water baptized. He did not list a long litany of offenses against God. He recognized the truth about Jesus, was humbled, and embraced that truth!

This is what each of us needs to do. We cannot give in to the lie that tells us that we are not good enough, or we have not given up enough before God will accept us. We must reject the lie that says we must somehow earn our salvation.

Jesus has done everything that is necessary to make salvation available to us. The only thing that is left for us is to see the truth.

Once we see that truth, it should humble us to the point of embracing Jesus and all that He stands for and is to us.

The eighth chapter of Romans begins with the fact that all who trust Jesus for salvation are no longer condemned...*ever*. All of my sins – past, present, and future – have not only been forgiven, but canceled. It is because of my faith in the atonement (death) of Jesus that God is able to cancel all of my sins, even the ones that I have not committed yet. This does not make me eager to commit them. It makes me want to do what I can to avoid sinning.

If you do not know Jesus, please do not put down this book without deliberately *believing* that He is God, that He died for you by the shedding of His blood on the cross, and that He rose three days later because death could not keep Him. Do you believe that? If you do not yet believe it, do you *want* to believe it? If so, then simply ask God to help you come to believe all that Jesus is and all that He has accomplished for you. God will answer your prayers and you may either receive instantaneous awareness of all that Jesus is and has done, or it may be a *growing* awareness over time. In either case, it is the most important decision you will ever make.

Turn to Him now and pray for knowledge of the truth and an ability to embrace it. Please. He is waiting for you.

Ask Yourself:

1. Do you *know* Jesus? Are you in *relationship* with Him? Have you had a spiritual transaction according to John 3?
2. Do you *want* to receive eternal life through the only salvation that is available?
3. Do you believe that Jesus is God the Son, who was born of a virgin, lived a sinless life, died a bloody and gruesome death to pay for your sin, was buried, and rose again on the third day? Do you *believe* this?
4. Do you *want* to *embrace* the truth from #3?

5. Pray that God will open your eyes and provide you with the faith to begin believing the truth about Jesus. Ask Him to help your faith embrace the truth, realizing that you are not good enough to save yourself and that your sin will keep you out of God's Kingdom without His salvation.
6. Pray as if your life depended upon it because *it does*!
7. If you have prayed to receive Jesus as Savior and Lord, please write to me. I want to send you some materials at *no charge or obligation*. Write to me at **fred_deruvo@hotmail.com** and sign up for our free bimonthly newsletter at **www.studygrowknow.com**

Visit our page on **OnePlace.com/ministries/study-grow-know** to hear our latest broadcasts as well as those that have been archived.

The Book of Jude

Society has changed drastically over the past decades. Why is that? Simply due to the fact that people have become more preoccupied with *Self*. In this book, Dr. Fred presents *Self* as an entity capable of getting things done its way and using the individual to accomplish it.

In essence, Self easily becomes the master to every person who is not under the control of God's Holy Spirit, with the person becoming the slave. ($14.99; 206 pages, 978-0983700630)

In this commentary on Revelation, author Fred DeRuvo draws back the curtain on chapters five through twenty-two, presenting information in an easy-to-understand style written for the average person. One thing is certain regarding the book of Revelation. Because of its prophetic nature, Christians will continue to debate aspects of it until such a time as we can know for certain. Either the things found within Revelation are yet to come to pass, and that alone will prove their veracity, or they will not come to *pass. Only time will tell.* ($18.00; 392 pages, 978-0977424498)

The Book of Jude

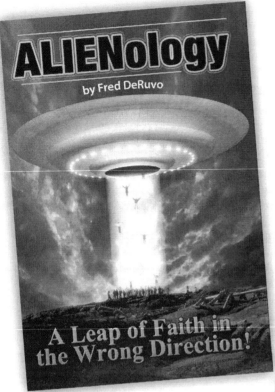

ALIENology is somewhat of a science for many who believe that entities from other planets or dimensions enter and leave our dimensions at will. What can we learn from these beings? Anything truthful? Dr. Fred believes that putting our faith in anything these beings say may be a huge leap in the wrong direction. Aliens reportedly come in all shapes, sizes, and even cultural representations. Because of this, there tends to be a good deal of mixed messages out there, yet people believe it because of their experience. Anything wrong with that picture? ($14.99; 176 pages, 978-0983700609)

Raised for His Glory delves into the books of Ezekiel and Romans to determine what the Bible actually says about Israel. Is the section on Ezekiel 36-39 speaking of a future time when nations will gather against Israel, or is this something that has already occurred? Moreover, just exactly what is the Valley of the Dry Bones referring to – the nation of Israel, or the Church? Join Dr. Fred as he presents his understanding of these very important sections of God's Word and how they relate to the only nation that He ever created, *Israel*. ($15.99; 190 pages, 978-0983700623)

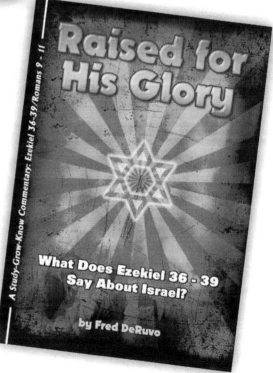

There is a chaos coming that is predicated upon the rise of Islam, Satanic Soldiers, aliens, and evil beyond measure. As an ideology, Islam masquerades as a religious light to the world, one that promises to usher in world peace – but at what cost? Through the use of political strategies, military might, and religious tenets, adherents of Islam work within various established governments to create special laws or exemptions for Muslims in the hope of eventually overthrowing that established government. Can it happen? IS it happening? Find out in *Evil Rising*. ($13.95; 184 pages, 978-0977424429)

We hear all the time how bad things are getting throughout the world. Do we chalk it all up to being the normal cycles that occur in life, or is something else going on behind the scenes? What if this generation alive now turns out to be the last one before Jesus returns? Is there any truth at all to the claim that Jesus will return one day? If you are one who has not taken the time to read through some of the books of the Bible that are said to teach truths regarding the last days, *Living in the Last Generation* puts it out there in a straightforward manner, making it easy to understand. ($11.95; 132 pages, ISBN: 978-0977424405)

Made in the USA
Charleston, SC
24 October 2011